JEANNE VICKERS

# Women and War

ZED BOOKS

*London & New Jersey*

*Women and War* was first published by Zed Books Ltd,
57 Caledonian Road, London N1 9BU and
165 First Avenue, Atlantic Highlands,
NJ 07716, USA in 1993.

Cover design by Andrew Corbett

Printed and bound in the United Kingdom
by Biddles Ltd, Guildford
and King's Lynn.

A catalogue record for this book is available
from the British Library

US cataloging-in-publication data is available
from the Library of Congress

ISBN 1 85649 229 X
ISBN 1 85649 230 3

# CONTENTS

Acknowledgments                                        vi
Preface, *Edith Ballantyne*                           vii

## 1. AN INTRODUCTION TO THE WAR GAME        1
A bellicose century                                    2
Civil war in Europe                                    5
Nuclear proliferation                                  7
Arms and the next generation                           9
Keeping the peace                                      12
The many forms of violence                             16

## 2. THE IMPACT OF WAR ON WOMEN             18
Women in the armed forces                              18
The prevalence of rape in wartime                      21
Caught in the crossfire                                23
The undefended                                         25
The uprooted                                           27
Women under apartheid                                  31
The Palestinians                                       32
Protection of the vulnerable                           35

## 3. THE CAUSES OF CONFLICT                 38
Militarism and militarization                          38
Weapons as status symbols                              41
Contributors to militarism                             43
The violence of maldevelopment                         46
A silent genocide                                      47

## 4. LESSONS OF THE GULF WAR                50
A United Nations war?                                  50
US aid to Iraq                                         54
The origins of the dispute                             55
Whose oil?                                             56
The social and economic costs                          57
The victims                                            59
Democracy in Kuwait and in Saudi Arabia                62
A hollow victory                                       64
The No-Fly Zone                                        65

## 5. WHAT CONSTITUTES SECURITY?                68

Arms and the environment                        69
Economic conversion                             73
Disarmament and development                     76
The 'peace dividend'                            79
European 'security clubs'                       81
UN moves towards arms control                   83
International intervention                      84

## 6. HUMAN RIGHTS AND GLOBAL SECURITY          88

Arms and the debt problem                       90
The right to food                               90
The health of a nation                          92
Educating women                                 93
Breadwinning women                              94
The plight of the homeless                      95
The question of equality                        95
Eliminating discrimination                      99

## 7. ACHIEVING VISIBILITY                      105

The roots of violence                           106
Sexual stereotypes                              107
Images in advertising                           108
Women's participation in decision-making        108
The invisibility problem                        111
The UN Commission on the Status of Women        113

## 8. WOMEN IN ACTION                           118

Peace Prizewinners                              119
Campaigning for peace                           120
Action at the grassroots                        122
Women in politics                               125
Writers and researchers                         126
The feminine approach to problem-solving        129

## 9. WORKING TOWARDS A NON-VIOLENT WORLD    133
Individual and collective rights    134
Political action groups    136
Education for peace    138
Games, toys and physical punishment    141
Textbooks and the media    142
Teaching conflict resolution    144
Peace camps and congresses    146

## 10. MAKING THE CONNECTION    149
Equal partnerships    149
The NGO framework    151
An agenda for action    153

## BOXES
One Woman's War Story    24
Arming the World    42
Nuclear Weapons Decision-making    45
An Environmental Budget    71
Hard-working Women    98
The Girl Child    102
The Violent Conflict Pyramid    128
Promoting Women in Chinese Society    152
Demystifying the Law    155

## ANNEXES
1  Selected Bibliography    159
2  Acronyms and abbreviations    163
3  Instruments and international agencies dealing
   with peace, security, and women in   development
   issues    165
4  Education Guide    169

Index    176

Cover photograph:  Living in the ruins of Vukovar, August
1992 (UNHCR/A. Hollmann)

# Acknowledgments

Because women and children are the first and foremost victims in wars and conflict situations, many women's non-governmental organizations have focused upon issues of war and peace in terms of their relationship to development and to economic and social justice. The dedicated activities of such groups have made a notable contribution to raising public awareness of the issues, but a great deal remains to be done and it is important that women continue to play a leading role in this area.

In 1987-88 I collaborated with members of the Joint UN/NGO Group on Women and Development in the production of a study kit entitled 'Women and Peace', prepared with the assistance of its consultant, Dr Betty Reardon, of Teachers College, Columbia University in New York.

Although the Group decided not to update this kit in the light of recent global developments, it seemed to me that the subject of women in relation to war was of vital importance, especially in view of the momentous changes which have taken place in the last few years and the ethnic rivalry and arms proliferation which are creating new and menacing dangers for humanity. I therefore decided to write a book which would take a fresh and purely personal look at the subject.

I wish to express my appreciation to the UN Non-Governmental Liaison Service (secretariat to the Women and Development Group), to the Lutheran World Federation, and to Edith Ballantyne, Secretary-General of the Women's International League for Peace and Freedom, for their advice and encouragement. I am also strongly indebted to Dr Reardon, a recognized leader in the field, whose research for the original study kit was invaluable. Her support has been warmly appreciated.

The opinions expressed in this volume are entirely my own, and should in no way be assumed to reflect the opinions of those mentioned above.

Please note that in this book 1 billion = 1,000 million, and 1 trillion = 1,000 billion.

**Jeanne Vickers**

# PREFACE: THOSE WHO UNDO ARMIES

In *Lysistrata*, a play written in 411 BC by the Greek philosopher, Aristophanes, the heroine's name means 'the one who undoes armies'.[1] At Lysistrata's instigation, the Acropolis and the treasury of Athens are seized by her followers on behalf of all the women of Greece, who declare a sex strike until such time as the men agree to bring the war to an end.

It is not suggested that late 20th-century women do likewise in order to enforce the settlement of disputes by means other than recourse to arms. It is, however, proposed that women, who with children are those who suffer most from wars, have far more power to stop them than most of them seem to think. This book is an investigation of the impact on women of war in general and in the most recent conflicts of the last decade, and a survey of the various ways in which women have worked and can contribute towards the peaceful settlement of confrontations between nations and communities.

It is clear that the end of the Cold War has in no way lessened the dangers of militarism but has rendered conflict, including nuclear confrontation, more likely and more uncontrollable. Security is not only a question of defence; the economic, social and environmental security of all is of vital importance if the threat of war is to be avoided. Economic espionage and trade wars at the macro level are only too likely to feed future upheavals and to lead to violence, as are hunger and deprivation at the micro level.

The author looks at many present-day wars and conflicts and their increasingly violent impact upon civilians, as well as at defence policies and the arms trade, the prospects for conversion from military to civilian production, and attempts by the United Nations to 'turn swords into ploughshares' through international peace-keeping and peace-making. The relationships between disarmament and development, and between peace and human rights, are also brought into focus.

It is of the utmost importance to women and men alike, and certainly to their children, that women play a greater role in the peaceful resolution of disputes in order that the 21st century may dawn in the light of new freedoms—freedom from insecurity, freedom from fear, freedom to fulfill the promise of a full and productive existence. Efforts to reduce militarism and the violent resolution of conflict must go hand in hand with development and the creation of a more just and equitable world.  In all of these areas the contribution of women can make all the difference.

It has taken a long time for women to begin to realize how important they are to the world's social and economic development.  Hopefully this book will help them to make the connection—between peace, stability, equality, and a truly just and equitable world order.

**Edith  Ballantyne**
President
Women's International League for
Peace and Freedom

---

1  Encyclopaedia Universales, p.2,657.

# 1. AN INTRODUCTION TO THE WAR GAME

> War's a game which
> were their subjects wise
> Kings would not play at
> William Cowper[1]

We live in strange times. On the one hand, the end of the Cold War and of the ideological confrontation between capitalism and communism has had a reverberating impact upon the whole international security environment. And on the other hand, the renewal of dormant antagonisms between states, and the emergence of new violence caused by ethnic and other tensions, have brought a new unpredictability to world affairs. It would seem that, in the closing years of the 20th century, it is nationalist fervour based upon ethnic, religious and cultural exclusivity, rather than liberal democracy, which will fill the vacuum created by the collapse of communism. While the tendency is for economic and technological forces to unify the world, ethnic quarrels threaten to split it apart.[2]

In his statement to the special meeting held in connection with Disarmament Week in October 1991 Javier Peréz de Cuéllar, then Secretary-General of the United Nations, called attention to the striking political changes in Europe and the gradual but steady resolution of numerous crises and conflict situations elsewhere. 'With the ideological confrontations and military competition of the cold war years having become obsolete, a comprehensive re-examination and revision of old doctrines and strategies that hindered progress towards arms reduction is a most natural development.'

At the same time, he said, 'even as the promise of further significant progress in arms limitation and disarmament has brightened considerably, the international situation remains unpredictable. The exacerbation of dormant tensions and the emergence of new clashes in certain areas of the world remind us how delicate the balance of security is and how much work remains to be done for strengthening the foundations of international peace and stability. It is also increasingly recognized that socio-economic and human rights questions bear as much on the issue of security as do military considerations. This poses an additional challenge to multilateral action in the areas of crisis prevention, conflict resolution and disarmament.' Mr Pérez de Cuéllar went on to point out that the development of objective, fair and workable criteria and guidelines to restrain the flow of conventional weapons and weapons technologies is sorely needed:

> The excessive militarization of human society, represented by unnecessarily high levels of armaments and military outlays, can no longer be condoned. Many of the countries which find themselves in this situation cannot afford either the human or the financial cost imposed by this process ... may I express my fervent hope that leaders everywhere will seize the opportunities opening now to make determined efforts to reverse the arms race and find new, cooperative ways to accomplish the increasingly-challenging tasks of building a better and more secure future for all societies.

## A bellicose century

According to Ruth Leger Sivard's *World Military and Social Expenditures 1991*, the 20th century's chapter in the history of warfare is unique. 'Wars now are shockingly more destructive and deadly. So far, in the 90 years of this century, there have been over four times as many war deaths as in the 400 years preceding.' And almost all the wars of the last two decades have been in the developing world.

The battlefields of 1990 in which annual deaths amounted to 1,000 or more included Afghanistan, Angola, Columbia, El Salvador, Ethiopia, Guatemala, India, Kuwait, Lebanon, Liberia, Mozambique, Peru, Somalia, South Africa, Sri Lanka, Sudan and Tibet. To these must now be added the Gulf War, and fighting in Yugoslavia and in several parts of the erstwhile Soviet Union. Sivard estimates that in 1988 there were no less than 111 organized armed conflicts (i.e sustained armed combat involving at least one government) taking place on the territory of 80 different countries, with at least 80 governments openly sending armed forces into battle. These conflicts may be grouped into three categories: classic wars pitting one government against another; wars of state formation, involving a government and an opposition group demanding autonomy or secession; and internal wars concerning the control of government within a given state.[3]

Under the main heading *The World's Wars* (sub-heading 'Tribalism revisited') the end-1991 London *Economist* reviewed the present state of world society and noted: 'War makes rattling good history;  but Peace is poor reading.  There's still plenty of rattling good history in the making, as well as some encouragingly poor reading'.

There have indeed been some encouraging developments with regard to some longstanding disputes, mainly due to more effective intervention by United Nations peace-keeping forces. War has ended in Nicaragua, and Namibia has won its independence. The UN has brokered peace negotiations in Angola, and continues to keep the lid on ethnic tensions in Cyprus. A peace agreement has been signed in El Salvador, ending the bloodiest battle fought in the Americas since the American Civil War, the death toll in which is estimated to have been 75,000 and the social and economic devastation beyond calculation.[4]

But civil strife continues in Sri Lanka, Peru and Guatemala, in Somalia, Sudan, Liberia and Mozambique; it breaks out intermittently in Chad, and is feared in Algeria, where Muslim radicals contest a military-backed government formed when democratic elections showed the Islamic Fundamentalist Party to be the probable winner. There is no longer war between Ethiopia and Eritrea, but in 1991, according to Tony Hickey, Coordinator of the Relief Society of Tigre, in London, 10,000 were dying every month and children as young as 13 were being pressed into the army, human rights abuses were rife, and torture of prisoners, political or criminal, was routine.[5]

In February 1992, at which time  some 1.8 million squatters displaced by drought and civil strife in southern Sudan had taken refuge in the capital, Khartoum, some 400,000 people, mainly women and children, were forced by the Sudanese government out of shelters and into a desert area devoid of food and water.

Violence in northwest Somalia and in its capital, Mogadishu, was estimated by the UN in February 1992 to have killed or wounded more than 20,000 people within ten weeks since heavy fighting resumed in November 1991 — the majority of them women and children. Combattants shelled the port of Mogadishu in February 1992 as a ship carrying 640 tons of

UN-supplied food was due to enter, forcing the ship to return to Kenya and leaving some 250,000 displaced people who had fled the embattled city totally without access to food, medical supplies, shelter or water.[6]

Meanwhile, armed groups established roadblocks to prevent food reaching the half a million Somali refugees in Eastern Ethiopia and the 375,000 Ethopian returnees in the Ogaden and in the south. In one refugee camp on the Kenyan border, according to the *Washington Post*, 5-10 Somalis were dying daily from pneumonia, tuberculosis, malaria or diarrhea. 'In all, 23 million people in eastern Africa are in harm's way because of war-aggravated starvation and disease.'[7]

And the tragedy goes on. In June 1992 it was reported by the UN High Commissioner for Refugees that 70 Somali refugees had been murdered by an armed gang on a ship that ran aground off Yemen, most of them women and children. Many of the women had been raped. In all, about 150 refugees had died after the ship, the *Gob Wein*, ran ground, having wandered the Gulf of Aden for two weeks with almost no food, water or medical assistance because local authorities in Yemen, overwhelmed by Somali refugees, had refused it entry. It is estimated by the International Committee of the Red Cross that fighting and famine have led to the flight of one in six from Somalia to neighbouring countries—about a million refugees.

The UN reports that mines may have killed 200,000 people during the 13-year-old Afghan civil war. Along with unexploded shells and bombs, they disabled about twice that number. The need for artificial limbs in this war-torn country is enormous. It is feared that the same situation will arise in Cambodia, where Khmer Rouge mines infest the landscape. Relief organizations say that Cambodia already has up to 30,000 amputees, victims of the land mines that were strewn throughout the country during 13 years of civil war.

In March 1992 it was estimated that up to half a million mines remained buried in three North-western provinces bordering Thailand; the rice planting season regularly becomes a 'mine injury epidemic' with as many as 500 amputations having to be performed. Rice planting is, of course, mainly women's work; Or Pram, aged 35 and mother of five, who lost a leg in the rice paddies of Siam Reap, is only one of many.[8]

As the Soviet Union disintegrated, fighting erupted in Georgia, Moldova and Ossetia, and escalated in Azerbaijan, where hunger came to the people of the secessionist Armenian enclave of Nagorno-Karabakh, blockaded and shelled for months by Azerbaijan forces. Not only did food supplies dwindle in the capital, Stepanakert, but antibotics, anaesthetics, intravenous fluids and electricity for X-rays became scarce or non-existent and at the few wells or streams in the city there were queues almost 24 hours a day. Reprisals by Armenia brought similar destruction upon the heads of the people of Azerbaijan. An attack by Azeri fighters on the Armenian village of Karin-Tak at the end of January 1992 killed 20 villagers and some 60 attackers, bringing the total killed in nearly four years of sporadic fighting to about 1,000 people.

## Civil war in Europe

Although there have been civil disturbances such as the terrorist activity still being carried out by the Basque movement ETA in Spain, and the long fratricidal struggle in Northern Ireland (which claimed 94 fatalities in 1991, 75 of them civilians), there had been only one civil war in Europe since World War II — that in Greece from 1946-49, in which more than 80,000 died — until tensions exploded in Yugoslavia as the 1990s began.

Civilians, and especially women and children, have been victimized in Yugoslavia, their homes and their livelihoods sacrificed on the altar of ethnic independence. Helsinki Watch, the US-based human rights group, reported in January 1992 that terrible atrocities had been committed by Serbian forces against Croatian civilians, and while these may not have been any worse than those committed by Croatian forces against Serbian civilians, such violence — which only exacerbated the basic political issues — soon spread to Bosnia-Herzogovina.

A Security Council embargo on Serbian-dominated Yugoslavia was imposed on 25 September 1991 in the light of constantly violated cease-fire agreements between the belligerents which had made it impossible to station UN peace-keepers. Fighting between Serbian and Bosnian forces put Sarajevo under siege for months, causing not only tremendous damage to the city but great hardship for the population under fire as food supplies dwindled and UN efforts to deliver relief supplies by air were hampered by bombardment of both city and airport.

In June 1992 human-rights monitors in Sarajevo put the toll at 50,000 or more dead, the great majority of them civilians, with some 600,000 driven from their homes by the fighting, and Blaine Harden reported in the 3 July 1992 edition of the *International Herald Tribune* that more than 1.4 million Bosnians, most of them Muslims, had been forced to leave their homes after scores of towns and villages in the east of the republic had been razed by Serbian forces. Efforts to halt the killing and destruction have included non-stop mediation by the EEC and the United Nations and the holding of an international conference in London in late August 1992.

Ethnic conflict is seen by Michael Clarke, director of the Centre for Defence Studies in London, to be the most likely problem of the politics of the 21st century. 'The doctrine of national self-determination, which has been a standard of the 20th century, is going to become the curse of the 21st.'[9] UN doctrine with regard to self-determination has hitherto been concerned with the granting of independence to colonial countries and peoples and the question of permanent sovereignty over natural resources, but will no doubt require further thought in view of the explosion of ethnic strife.[10]

In fact, the situation is even more complex, for the peoples fighting each other in Bosnia-Herzogovina—Orthodox Serbs, Catholic Croats and Islamic Bosnians—belong to the same ethnic and linguistic group but have different religious and cultural affiliations. If the fighting spreads, it could involve Muslims in Kosovo and Albania, and Orthodox Macedonians. The Royal Institute of International Affairs in London has estimated that there are 125 ethnic or minority disputes in the former Soviet Union alone, including the fight between Christian Armenians and Muslim Azerbaijanis.

The question of self-determination was raised by Antoine Blanca, UN Under-Secretary-General for Human Rights, at an August 1992 meeting in Geneva in the following terms:

> The right of peoples to self-determination was enshrined under the Charter. Yet if every racial, national, ethnic or linguistic group claimed statehood, the resulting fragmentation would make peace, security, economic well-being and the observance of human rights more difficult to achieve. In this context, the promotion of a deeper sensitivity to the rights of minorities and of a firm

commitment to counter racist violence and discrimination become all the more necessary.

As the *Economist* pointed out in its 8 February 1992 issue, the end of the Cold War does not mean a world at peace. 'On the contrary, it may for a time mean an even more violent world, as the sort of local tough who used to shelter under a superpower's protection now finds that he can survive only by the power of his own fist. These people will be the main danger to international order in the next few years ... None of them will wield anything like the power the Soviet Union once wielded, but some of them will be militarily strong enough to ignore mere diplomatic disapproval or an economic slap on the wrist. This requires, among other things, urgent action about nuclear weapons.'

## Nuclear proliferation

Indeed, it was already clear by the end of the 1980s that new thinking with regard to non-proliferation was urgently needed, new thinking made even more difficult by a US refusal to support a comprehensive test ban treaty. Speaking at a United Nations meeting on disarmament in Geneva in February 1992, Russian Foreign Minister Andrei Kozyrev called for a 'fundamental revision of military nuclear doctrines worldwide', and suggested that Moscow and Washington should lead the move.

The fragile, unstable world which emerged from the break-up of the Soviet Union into independent states, and the overthrow of communist régimes in Eastern Europe, has in no way reduced the nightmare of possible nuclear proliferation. The end of the Cold War, and the dire economic circumstances in which the Commonwealth of Independent States finds itself, mean that the situation is no longer under control and that there is no money to fund destruction of such weapons. One result is that a great many scientists, and large quantities of weapons, are likely to find themselves in great demand by countries wishing to build up a nuclear and conventional armaments capacity.

Already, Iran has bought at least two newly built Russian attack submarines. With the Pentagon budget falling, American arms salesmen are prowling for customers such as Saudi Arabia, which wants to buy 24 McDonnell Douglas F-15E fighters to transform its air force into one that could meet threats from nuclear submarines. 'It would indeed be tragic if the end of the Cold War and the Gulf War were to set off a whole series of arms races around this defiled and lovely planet,' said a leader writer in *The Baltimore Sun* in February 1992.[11]

The danger is recognized. Several suggestions have been made for an urgent attempt to use unemployed Russian scientists in other, more benign, industries, and the need to strengthen the power of the International Atomic Energy Agency's (IAEA) inspection procedures is considered essential. But the IAEA, under present rules, cannot inspect a country's nuclear facilities unless that country has adhered to the UN's Treaty on Non-Proliferation of Nuclear Weapons (NPT).

The same would probably apply to the creation of an international monitoring agency under the auspices of the UN in order to encourage compliance and assure that no government could avoid detection of violations, although one suggestion is for such an agency to utilize surveillance by high altitude aircraft, satellites, and similar means.

There is a new recognition of the need for strict control over stockpiles and prevention of their accidental or unauthorized use — a question which, in today's volatile world, has acquired an urgent dimension — and an increase in efforts to prevent their proliferation. Although a UN team of experts in Iraq encountered great difficulty in locating and destroying that country's military stockpile, Syria in February 1992 consented to inspection of its nuclear facilities by the IAEA. The Agency inspected those of Iran and came to the conclusion that its nuclear power is for peaceful purposes only.

In November 1990 the presidents of Argentina and Brazil ended years of secret military efforts to build a bomb by signing an agreement renouncing the manufacture of nuclear weapons, and envisaging negotiations with the IAEA to set up a system of international safeguards and inspections of their nuclear installations. A few months later France announced a temporary suspension of nuclear testing in the Pacific.

Alas, the Latin American example is not being followed by some other countries, notably in Asia. A report in the *International Herald Tribune* of 15 February 1992 indicated that India insisted upon the right to build nuclear weapons: 'We are determined to retain our status as a peaceful nuclear state with the option to build weapons in accordance with our threat perception', said an official report. At the same time Pakistan announced that it had the capability to build at least one nuclear device.

Both American and European intelligence officials have reported that Israel is close to developing submarine-launched nuclear-armed cruise missiles, a potentially catastrophic development for the stability of the region. Although Israel's attack against Iraq's IAEA-approved Osirak reactor was condemned by the UN Security Council as a violation of the UN charter and a threat to the non-proliferation treaty/IAEA régime, there is no sign of such condemnation with regard to Israel's own nuclear weapons production.

According to Jennifer Scarlott, writing in the *World Policy Journal*, in order to effectively curb proliferation in the post Cold-War era it will be necessary to abandon both the traditional NPT régime and the highly militarized approach of the Bush administration. 'What is needed is a cooperative, more equitable approach to the problem that tries to address the roots of nuclear proliferation in political conflict, economic disparities, and insecurity ... Perhaps most important of all will be efforts to redraw ... the pledge that the hierarchical international order on which the Treaty rested would provide a minimum of peace and stability. What is needed in place of a world of nuclear "haves" and "have-nots" is one in which all states agree to give up some of their sovereign prerogatives for the greater good.'

Scarlott insists that, if the countries of the world are to build a new, more cooperative international system hospitable to non-proliferation efforts, 'it is essential that the United States recognize that it is neither desirable nor possible for it to serve as a global police officer. That task must rest with the United Nations, or with whichever international institution a majority of nation-states endows with the mandate and legitimacy to act in their collective name'.[12]

## Arms and the next generation

Meanwhile, vast sums continue to be spent on armaments. In recent decades military expenditures have absorbed five per cent of all goods and services produced in the world, five times more than the percentage allocated to defence before the second world war, and 15-20 per cent of central government revenues and expenditures—three times their budgets for education, eight times that for housing.[13]

Governments are investing 30 times more per member of the armed forces than they invest in the education of a child enrolled in school. This is purely negative expenditure, given the fact that weapons can only be used in war or become obsolete; it is investment at the expense of positive expenditure, i.e. in human capital through economic and social development. And although the most severe educational shortfall is in the developing world, where large numbers of children are deprived of even minimal

**Average military spending around the world, 1972-88**

as a percentage of:

| | GDP 1972-88 | World military expenditure 1972-88 | Central govt. expenditure 1972-88 |
|---|---|---|---|
| Industrial countries | 3.8 | 52.7 | 14.3 |
| Eastern Europe | 9.2 | 25.4 | 20.7 |
| Developing countries | 5.9 | 22.0 | 20.0 |
| Asian developing | 6.3 | 8.1 | 27.2 |
| Middle East | 11.6 | 8.0 | 23.1 |
| North Africa | 9.6 | 1.8 | 17.1 |
| Sub-Saharan Africa | 3.7 | 1.5 | 12.8 |
| Latin-America and Caribbean | 2.3 | 2.5 | 8.6 |
| Total: | 4.9 | 100.00 | 16.5 |

Source: *Finance & Development*, September 1991.

schooling, and adult illiteracy is growing, in the so-called developed countries education has long been accorded too low a priority as compared with defence.

Yet in the major industrial countries, high military expenditures are associated with low growth in productivity—in the US, an annual rate of 2.8 per cent, in the ex-USSR, just 2.4 per cent. Japan, with its military budget consuming only a low 0.9 per cent of GNP (gross national product), has seen an annual average rise in productivity of 7.8 per cent, with consequently rapid economic growth. Although US Congressmen battle to save defence contracts which provide employment in their districts, for example the Seawolf submarine and the F.14 fighter plane, opinion polls show strong popular support for diverting military dollars to domestic programmes as recognition grows that such expenditures stand in the way of improvements in highway construction, education, and the social fabric of the nation.[14]

On 8 March 1991 the UN Conference on Disarmament in Geneva was presented with an International Women's Day statement by participants in a Women's Conference which had just taken place at the Palais des Nations. It laid stress on the fact that the Gulf War had underscored the importance of progress on the critical issues before the Conference. These included the need for the speedy conclusion of the convention on chemical weapons and for their destruction, for nuclear disarmament, and for the conclusion of a binding international instrument prohibiting attacks on nuclear facilities as potential radiological weapons.

Pointing to the enormous damage that weapons and war inflict upon the environment, and the fact that the world is facing a serious ecological crisis, the statement insisted that inadequate attention was being paid to the real and potential environmental costs of all types of weaponry, and indicated their deep concern for the future, both for their children and for the planet. The goal of general and complete disarmament was not a utopian dream but a global imperative, to build just relations and to release the resources necessary to respond to the ecological and development crises that threaten to steal the future. It was the responsibility of the Disarmament Conference to negotiate disarmament agreements that would help to usher in a safe and secure future, free from the menace of weapons of mass destruction, and to insist that global relations must be based not on military force but on cooperation.[15]

So far as chemical weapons are concerned, it would appear that progress is being made. A draft text of a treaty to ban chemical weapons, subject to approval by the UN General Assembly, was declared ready in June 1992, the first complete, multilaterally negotiated text since the negotiations began 24 years ago in 1968 to try to ban not just the use, currently prohibited, but also the production and stockpiling of poison gas.

## Keeping the peace

Peace-keeping has been one of the more successful activities of the United Nations. It can only be undertaken as an expression of international political consensus and will, and with an undivided Security Council. The Secretary-General cannot permit himself to support—or even to give the impression of supporting—one of the parties to a conflict, since peace-keeping operations are based on the consent and the cooperation of all interested parties.

While there have been a number of successful operations in which UN forces have been able to keep the peace between the two sides and so give negotiation a chance, this pattern was broken in the case of the Gulf War—a disastrous departure which is the subject of Chapter 4. Now there are voices (for example, that of Bernard Kouchner, French Minister for Health and Humanitarian Action) raised in favour of far more action on the part of the UN in the area of preventive diplomacy and peace-making, as preliminaries to peace-keeping.

Brian Urquhart and Erskine Childers, retired senior officials of the United Nations, in a study envisaging the future shape of the world body, have pointed out that 'peace and security are increasingly an indispensable complement of the resolution of the world's economic, ecological and social problems, which have themselves become security problems.'[16] Urquhart, former UN Under-Secretary-General in charge of peace-keeping, has suggested that a new category of international military operation is needed which would involve an element of intervention in order to bring violence under control and provide an atmosphere in which the conciliation process could go forward.

These operations would essentially be armed police actions, for which a wide range of governments would have to be willing to provide highly trained and well-led military contingents under UN command so that the Security Council could deploy an international force quickly in a situation where the cycle of violence could not be broken except by firm intervention.[17]

Whether this controversial suggestion can get off the ground is open to question, given that international intervention in most forms is, after the Gulf War, extremely suspect in many parts of the world. However, in a June 1992 report entitled *An Agenda for Peace* UN Secretary-General Boutros Boutros-Ghali called for a new approach involving preventive deployment, early warning of potential conflicts, peace enforcement units, optional UN military action, post-combat confidence-building, and greater reliance upon the International Court of Justice for peaceful adjudication of disputes.

It is clear that new UN controls will have to be devised if violence between states or ethnic communities continues to pose a threat, not only to themselves but to the rest of humanity. It is also clear that the use of force to demonstrate power or superiority, as a means to compel frontier revision or to maintain social order, must eventually be outlawed by the international community.

Former US Defense Secretary James R. Schlesinger has written that American society must recast its definition of power to include such elements as economic competitiveness, productivity and investment in industry, which he suggested would move to more commanding positions as the need for massive military strength disappears. But Representative Les Aspin, Democrat of Wisconsin and chairman of the House Armed Services Commitee, has suggested that the Gulf War should be the model for future wars; the Iraq experience 'would be transplanted around the globe to measure the relative strength of other troublesome regional powers as a means to plan forces to defeat them'—a method dubbed by Mr. Aspin 'Iraq equivalents'.

A 'unipolarist' school of thought now seems to be emerging within US policy circles, according to an article by Charles Krauthammer in the journal *Foreign Affairs*: 'The United States is now the sole superpower, these analysts argue, and the only country capable of leading the fight against aggression and instability around the world ... there is no alternative to confronting, deterring and, if necessary, disarming states that brandish and use weapons of mass destruction. And there is no one to do that but the United States, backed by as many allies as will join the endeavour ... The alternative to unipolarity is chaos.'[18] Mention of the UN is conspicuous by its absence.

Although both the United States and the United Kingdom plan to reduce troop strengths, the frustration of the military, and the power of the military-industrial complex, have resulted in efforts to maintain military expenditures in the United States at present levels or not far below them, and a determination to produce new and more powerful weapons, if only as 'pilot models'. In February 1992 Pentagon planning documents were made available to *New York Times* reporter Patrick E. Tyler 'by an official who wished to call attention to what he considered vigorous attempts within the military establishment to invent a menu of alarming war scenarios that can be used by the Pentagon to prevent further reductions in forces or cancellations of new weapon systems from defense contractors'.

The leaked documents, which seemed to espouse the 'unipolarist' approach, outlined seven 'scenarios' for potential foreign conflicts which could draw US forces into combat during the next ten years, including individual and simultaneous attacks against Iraq and North Korea, a major military campaign in Europe against a resurgent Russia, intervention against a military coup in the Philippines and a 'narco-terrorist' plot threatening access to the Panama Canal, and, finally, a strategy to deter the re-emergence later in this decade of a global 'adversarial rival' or 'international coalition with an aggressive expansionist security policy.'

According to Tyler, the Pentagon considered the scenarios 'illustrative, not predictive.' But, he noted, the new documents 'suggest levels of manpower and weapons that would appear to stall, if not reverse, the downward trend in defense spending by mid-decade. They indicate that although the Pentagon has abandoned planning for a superpower military confrontation after the collapse of the Soviet Union and the end of the Cold War, it is not yet prepared to consider drastically reduced force levels ... for example, the United States would need to keep aircraft carriers and their escort warships dispersed around the world to deal with potential trouble from the Baltic Sea to the South China Sea, a requirement that would support the Navy's assertion that it needs 12 carrier battle groups.'[19]

The documents aroused so much public alarm that the final Pentagon recommendations were considerably modified. It is clear, however, that the military mind-set has not changed, and that such scenarios would be strongly supported by industries and States likely to be affected by arms reductions. There is thus likely to be considerable, though muted, opposition to the agreement on far-reaching cuts in strategic and other weaponry reached by US President Bush and Russian President Yeltsin in Washington in June 1992.

At the end of January 1992, under the presidency of Prime Minister John Major of the United Kingdom and with Russia replacing the former Soviet Union, the Security Council met in special session and at the highest level to reaffirm its commitment to peace-keeping and to peace-making. Explaining at a press conference the statement, which had been unanimously adopted by the Council, Major said:

> In it, we pledge ourselves to collective security, inter-. national law and our commitments under the United Nations Charter: to resolve disputes peacefully; to fight against terrorism; to pursue arms control, disarmament and non-proliferation; and to conclude a chemical weapons convention in 1992. That statement, as ever, is written in the polite language of diplomacy, but it contains a hard cutting edge that can be used against those who breach their obligations.

The statement included *inter alia* references to strengthening United Nations action in preventive diplomacy, peace-keeping and peace-making, and to human rights verification, to progress in democracy and responsive forms of government, to election monitoring, and to the promotion of a better life for all in larger freedom. It did not, however, go into one important detail: the question of cost. Simultaneous UN requests for 15,000 peace-keeping troops for Cambodia and 14,000 for Yugoslavia in March 1992 brought that detail into sharp focus as the US Congress reacted with hostility to Secretary of State James Baker's request for $800 million to meet its part of the cost of deploying those troops. And yet, as noted in a *New York Times* editorial, in hard cash terms UN peace-keeping is a bargain:

> Each day of Operation Desert Storm cost $1.5 billion. The US share for a year of expanded UN peace-keeping is a fraction of Pentagon expenditures for weapons that will not be used against a Soviet adversary that no longer exists. Every war prevented saves blood and treasure, expands markets and trade. Peace in Angola, El Salvador, Yugoslavia or Cambodia is a boon to all but the arms bazaar.

As the editorialist pointed out, the peace-keepers are now doing more than monitoring truce lines, they are becoming peace-makers too. 'UN forces were asked to disarm guerrillas, conduct elections and enforce human rights, first in Namibia, then in Cambodia and El Salvador. The Security Council recently expanded the concept of threats to peace to include economic, social and ecological instability ... Why couldn't the United States, which now owes $377 million in back dues for peacekeeping, meet part of its obligation through the defense budget? ... What a chance for President George Bush to take the lead in giving real meaning to his still hazy vision of a "new world order"!'[20]

## The many forms of violence

Violence in our daily lives can take many forms, ranging from family disputes, corporal punishment, aggressive and criminal attacks on individuals, torture in detention, terrorism and kidnapping, vicious forms of local gang warfare, all the way to the highly sophisticated and destructive weapons now used in international combat, as for example in the Gulf War. There is also the structural violence of poverty and underdevelopment, which denies basic human rights and condemns millions to deprivation, hunger, disease, illiteracy, unemployment and alienation—a potent breeding ground for conflict.[21]

In every one of these cases human beings are subjected to personal aggression, but in none so mindlessly and indiscriminately as in wars, insurrections, or battles for secession or independence, which involve whole communities and result not only in the death and injury of civilians but in the loss of income, homes, and family support. And in every one of these cases the majority of victims are women and children.

---

1   Cowper, William, 'The Winter Morning Walk', *The Task* (1785).

2   S.Rajaratnam, former foreign minister of Singapore, in 'The Ethnic Fires won't die out', *International Herald Tribune (IHT)*, 12/1/91.

3   Commission of the Churches on International Affairs, *Disarmament Prospects and Problems*. Background Information, 1990/2, World Council of Churches, Geneva.

4   *IHT* editorial, 21/1/92.

5   Letter to the *IHT*, 4/2/92.

6   Report in the *IHT*, 8-9/2/92.

7   Reprinted in the *IHT*, 19/2/92

8   *UN Secretariat News*, February 1992.

9   As reported by Eugene Robinson in the *IHT*, in August 1992.

10   See: UN Declaration on the Granting of Independence to Colonial Countries and Peoples, GA resolution 1514 (XV) of 14/12/60; also GA resolution 1803 (XVII) of 14/12/62 on permanent sovereignty over natural resources.

11   Quoted in the *IHT*, 12/2/92.

12   Jennifer Scarlott, 'Nuclear Proliferation after the Cold War', in*World Policy Journal*, Vol.VIII, No.4, Fall 1991.

13   Commission of the Churches on International Affairs, op.cit.

14   As reported by Eric Schmitt, *IHT* 13/2/92.

15   UN press release DC/1715, March 1991.

16   Brian Urquhart and Erskine Childers, *A World In Need of Leadership: Tomorrow's United Nations*, Dag Hammarskjöld Foundation, Uppsala, Sweden (1990) p.21.

17   Brian Urquhart, 'How the United Nations could break up civil wars', *IHT*, 31/12/1991-1/1/1992.

18   Charles Krauthammer, 'The Unipolar Moment', *Foreign Affairs*, quoted by Jennifer Scarlott, op.cit.

19   Patrick E. Tyler, *New York Times Service*, in the *IHT*, 18/2/92.

20   Reprinted in the *IHT*, 7-8/3/92.

21   Structural violence as a concept was first defined by the Norwegian peace researcher Johan Galtung in 1967.

# 2. THE IMPACT OF WAR ON WOMEN

> What difference does it make to the dead, the orphans and the homeless, whether the mad destruction is wrought under the name of totalitarianism or the holy name of liberty or democracy?
>
> Mohandas K. Gandhi[1]

Left to sustain the family and endure the loneliness and vulnerability of separation, women suffer great hardships in wartime. They, and those they care for, may be killed or injured in ethnic fighting or civil disturbances in spite of being innocent bystanders. Their houses may be damaged, or they may flee from home in fear of their lives. Dwindling food supplies and hungry children exacerbate tensions. And so, to the loss of husbands, fathers, sons and brothers who are killed in battle, is added the longer-term suffering of further deprivation.

Often defenceless against invasion, women can find that armed conflict means rape and other forms of abuse by occupying troops, as well as loss of the means of livelihood. Rural women must carry additional responsibilities while their menfolk are absent, left to tend both to their farms and domestic needs, and many have been the cases in which women farmers have lost their crops first to occupying troops and then to their own.

## Women in the armed forces

Others are recruited into the armed services, usually occupying 'base' or menial positions such as cooks and drivers, secretaries or in some more ornamental role. Although women's service in the armed forces is usually depicted by governments as a matter of 'equality', it is rare indeed that women climb out of the ranks. Some 20,000 women were involved in the Gulf War; they were excluded from combat duties but allowed to launch Patriot missiles, and so became direct perpetrators of violence. Although Boulding[2] has suggested that women infiltrate the military in order to change it, the more likely result is that militarization will change women.

In any event, women's influence in and upon the military is likely to remain minimal for so long as they continue to be subject to discrimination and to sexual harassment. A study by a retired US Navy officer, Kay Krohne, asserts that sexual harassment is widespread in the Navy but that many women are fearful of reporting it. Her findings parallel a 1990 US Defense Department report which found that 64 per cent of women in the US military had been sexually harassed.[3] And although women have often played important roles in resistance movements, the men in those movements have often proved to be as ambivalent about women's roles as are the military.[4]

Curiously, the situation was very different in the 19th century. The Austrian and Italian armies regularly commissioned women soldiers who saw action and received the highest decorations. Augusta Krüger of the Ninth Prussian Regiment was decorated both with the Iron Cross and the Russian Order of St George. In France, Angélique Brulon, sub-lieutenant of the infantry, was decorated with the Légion of Honour, while dragoon Thérèse Figuer had four horses killed under her but died in her bed at the age of 87. Many women fought in the American Civil War.[5]

Women have taken up arms to end colonial rule or to participate in wars of liberation or partisan struggles which are often the consequence of people's lack of basic necessities as well as an attempt to gain freedom from oppression. They have even been terrorists—or freedom-fighters, depending upon one's perspective. Women and young girls are known to have taken part in some 20 wars in recent years, as soldiers or as military support forces, and have been part of the action in South Africa, Mozambique, El Salvador, Guatemala, Peru, Sri Lanka, the Philippines, and with Palestinian fighters in Lebanon and the Israeli-occupied territories.

In Lebanon, where neighbourhoods have been on the front line for many years, women on all sides took part mainly by providing food to combatants, sewing hospital sheets, administering first aid, and donating blood. Che Guevara, in his book on guerrilla warfare, writes that among the worst things during the Cuban war was the fact that the guerrillas were forced to eat the tasteless and sticky food that, in the absence of women, they had to make themselves.[6]

Women have always been part of the human rights struggle, although usually in a non-violent fashion, as in Chile and

*Mothers 1 ru*

Argentina where they caught world attention in their efforts to obtain the liberation of those who had 'disappeared'. But, like men, women can suffer brutal abuse if they defy their governments or insist on their rights; in many countries such rights activists have been subject to arbitrary arrest and torture and have been judicially executed or murdered by government agents.

A recent Amnesty International report says that in June 1989, when Chinese troops attacked demonstrators in Tienenmen Square, an armoured personnel carrier ploughed right over one of the temporary tents erected by the students, killing the seven girls inside. Dan Jing, a woman journalist working with *New China News*, was arrested and forced to perform hard labour. Wang Zhihong was arrested in November 1989 while on an escape route to Hong Kong; eight months pregnant, she gave birth prematurely in prison and her child did not survive.[7]

In armed conflicts women and their families are not immune to government repression and the denial of human rights. As prisoners of war they have often been victimized as women — indeed, the world's torturers, executioners and jailers do not discriminate on grounds of sex, says Amnesty:

> Women are as likely as men to suffer brutal abuses if they question the *status quo*, defy their governments or insist on their rights. In different countries with differing ideologies, women have been killed by the authorities, judicially executed or murdered by government agents. At least 24 of the 36 people stoned to death in Iran in 1989 were women, sentenced to this particularly cruel punishment for offences such as adultery or prostitution
> ...
> Women as well as men spend years in prison after being convicted in unfair trials. Carole Richardson spent 15 years in a British prison because she was convicted on the basis of an uncorroborated 'confession' made under duress while she was held incommunicado. She was arrested when she was a child of 17. In 1975 she was sentenced to life imprisonment for two bombings. She was released in 1989, when it emerged that she and her three co-defendants, known as the Guildford Four, had been wrongly convicted because of police malpractice

which included lying to the court about the confession statements ...

Hundreds, if not thousands, of women are prisoners of conscience, detained for their peaceful opposition to the authorities, sometimes without having been charged or brought to trial.[8]

## The prevalence of rape in wartime

Rape in war and civil disturbance seems endemic. In counter-insurgency operations, government soldiers sometimes use rape and sexual abuse to try to extract information from women suspected of involvement with the armed opposition or even to punish women who simply live in areas known to be sympathetic to the insurgents. Official failure to condemn or punish rape gives it an overt political sanction, which allows rape and other forms of torture and ill-treatment to become tools of military strategy.

The Japanese Prime Minister Kiichi Miyazawa, on a recent visit to South Korea, found that Korean women had long memories. During World War II the Japanese Army forced Korean women to serve Japanese soldiers as prostitutes, and women turned out in large numbers to protest against his visit. Among them was one sent to a Japanese naval base at the age of 16 and forced to undergo intercourse 10 to 15 times a day, every day. She was regularly beaten and once stabbed. Eventually she returned to Korea but she was too ashamed to marry or even go back to her family.[9]

Following a formal apology by the Japanese government, whose military documents linked the former Imperial Army to the recruitment and management of 'comfort girls', Mr Miyazawa apologised personally: 'I would like to express my apologies and remorse to all those people who experienced indescribable sufferings as so-called field comfort women', he told South Korean journalists prior to his three-day visit to Séoul. In July 1992 the Japanese government finally admitted that its military forced tens of thousands of women to work in a vast network of government-run brothels to provide sex for Japanese soldiers during World War II.[10]

But the Japanese have not been the only ones to use 'comfort women'. Originally a small fishing village, Olongapo in the

Philippines became a city enriched by the earnings of some 700 clubs and bars that catered to hundreds of thousands of US marines and sailors at the US Subic Bay naval base. Some 16,000 women mobilized to be at their service came from brothels in nearby Subic town where they lived virtually in white slavery.[11]

Among many examples quoted by Amnesty, Columbian troops arrested pregnant 15-year-old Sandra Patricia Vélez near her home in Yondo in February 1989; her body was found in September 1990 in a shallow grave. Peruvian security forces appear to act with impunity in committing rape and other forms of torture or ill-treatment, their victims including leaders of women's groups, teachers, and the wives of suspected government opponents.

Soldiers in Myanmar are said to have raped women, including an 11-year-old girl, as punishment for disobeying official regulations, or taken them hostage while they searched for suspected political opponents.   And a para-military group in the Philippines reportedly took into custody two women belonging to the Alliance of Poor Farmers, Marilyn Negro and Teresita Udtohan, six months pregnant. Their mutiliated bodies were found two months later.

In Bangladesh tribal women in the Chittagong Hill Tracts are said to have been raped by members of the security forces in apparent reprisal attacks against the men of the community, some of whom are active in armed movements for regional autonomy, and a 17-year-old girl was brutally raped by a number of soldiers because her brother was suspected of being a political activist. A 40-year-old woman said: 'While some pinned us down the others raped us. We had already heard the sounds of bullets and the screams of our men being beaten up. So we did not have any courage to protest and had to meekly surrender to the torture.'[12]

In Turkey it is reported that rape and sexual abuse are frequently used in attempts to extract confessions from both men and women during interrogation. A 20-year-old Turkish university student, arrested in May 1991 and accused of complicity in the murder of a Regional Commander, was repeatedly stripped, hung up by her wrists with leather straps, laid naked on blocks of ice and tortured with electric shocks, and sexually molested. Although innocent, she signed a prepared confession which she was not allowed to read.[13]

Mauritanian soldiers are reported to have raped young women from the village of Toumbel in June 1989, then forced them to cross the river into Senegal naked. A 25-year-old woman held for three months in a Nouakchott police station says that she was raped by soldiers at the post for an entire night before being expelled and thrown into the Senegal River. And in November 1989 three members of the National Guard fired on a group of women and children outside their village of Nere-Walo in the Kaedi area of southern Mauritania, killing a young woman and two children.[14]

Mothers and children attempting to flee from the fighting in northwest Somalia have been detained and killed by the military, and were victims of extrajudicial executions in other areas as fighting escalated in 1989 and 1990. In Azerbaijan (ex-USSR), according to news reports, two Armenian women were allegedly thrown to their deaths from a high building, and one pregnant woman burned alive, in an attack by Azeris.

Reports of arbitrary arrest, torture, rape and killing followed the Iraqi invasion of Kuwait in August 1990, and a 25-year-old woman, who was shot in the head when troops opened fire on a group of women and young people protesting against the invasion, died later in hospital. During the week following the invasion Iraqi soldiers are said to have raped three Filipino women and a British woman held in their custody. The Iraqi authorities apparently detained women, as well as men and children, for offences such as possession of opposition literature or the Kuwait flag—offences punishable by execution.[15]

Horrifying stories emerged from Bosnia-Herzogovina in late 1992 concerning the rape and deliberate impregnation of thousands of women, mostly Muslims violated by Serbian soldiers, as a form of 'ethnic cleansing'. United Nations human rights authorities are looking into the allegations, while UNICEF and other UN bodies are studying ways of helping the victims and their babies. International women's groups are demanding that the perpetrators be brought before the United Nations War Crimes Commission.

## Caught in the crossfire

But rape, torture and killing are not the only horrors suffered by women in times of conflict. Most women's experience of war is not as combatants or activists but as civilians caught in the crossfire. While exact figures are hard to find, it is clear that the percentage of civilians killed or disabled in warfare is climbing sharply. According to studies undertaken for the International Symposium on Children and War held in Finland in 1983, among the casualties in World War II civilians represented 50 per cent, a ratio now exceeding 80 per cent. In the hostilities in Lebanon civilians are estimated to have accounted for more than 90 per cent of the deaths, a significant majority of these being women and children.[16]

A similar toll is likely to emerge from the civil war in Yugoslavia. On 6 December 1991 James Grant, Executive Dorector of the United Nations Children's Fund (UNICEF), issued a plea for the protection and safety of women and children trapped in the fierce fighting in the ancient city of

---

### ONE WOMAN'S WAR STORY

Yugoslavia today is a place of deep cellars and shallow graves. Marica Racimorski, a recently widowed Croat, knows about both. For when a country is torn apart, families do the bleeding.

Marica's younger son, Vinko, fled to live with his wife's parents in Serbia when hostilities broke out, and was promptly conscripted by the federal army and sent to join the siege of his hometown, Vukovar, the Croatian city where his mother was born and the family lived. Her elder son, Zlatko, was seriously wounded while defending Vukovar and is now in the intensive-care ward of a Zagreb hospital. Her husband, Ivan, was wounded in November while on his way to visit Zlatko, then in a Vukovar hospital, developed gangrene and died.

Marica, her hair now white, survived by moving from cellar to cellar, protected by Vukovar's accumulated rubble. Her 4-bedroom house had been destroyed, and every house in her street heavily damaged by tank fire. When she went to see Zlatko, bent in half to avoid bullets, she had to cross a graveyard which stank. The bodies, mostly those of Croat and Serb civilians, had not been buried very deep, and the air was unhealthy for survivors.

In Zagreb, Marica learned that Vinko and his father-in-law had found her husband in the Vukovar hospital morgue, and had buried him, deep, in what is known as the Bulgarian cemetery. But she probably will not visit his grave. She doesn't know if she can bear to return to Vukovar.[17]

Dubrovnik, while UNESCO undertook a special mission to try to prevent extensive damage to a city so beautiful, according to the *Christian Science Monitor,* that 'even Napoleon is said to have vowed to spare it in battles for the Dalmatian Coast'. The lovely ancient city of Mostar has been reduced to rubble, and mass graves were found there at the end of August 1992.[18] Extensive damage to the Bosnian city of Sarajevo has victimized desperate women seeking food and shelter for their families.

In November 1991, according to Amnesty, Yugoslav federal army troops and Serbian paramilitiaries attacked and searched the villages of Skabrnja and Nadin near Zadar, and fleeing villagers reported a massacre of civilians. A list of 45 dead later compiled by the pathology department of Zadar hospital concluded that all except 14 had died from a single close-range gunshot wound—among them six women aged between 40 and 70.[19] Such atrocities add to the horror behind reports concerning Serbia's genocidal policy of 'ethnic cleansing' of conquered territories.

## The undefended

Women suffer greatly in their traditional roles as homemakers, mothers and care-givers in times of conflict, losing the support of husbands and sons who join the fighting, seeing their young children and aged parents go hungry when food supplies and other necessities are destroyed or sent to the war zones, and when basic necessities like bread become unobtainable. Inevitably, they deprive themselves in order to give to others. In societies where women's status and welfare depend upon their relationship to men, widows are often left without means to provide for themselves and their children; and thousands were effectively 'widowed' when their husbands 'disappeared' after being held in custody:

Women in this position are doubly punished ... Not only have they lost their husbands, but as their husbands are not legally dead they cannot claim state or other benefits. ... The price 22-year-old Carmela Ferro Estrada paid for asking too many questions about her husband's 'disappearance' was being forced to give birth to her third child in prison [while] Maria Guinarita Pisco Pisango paid with her life for the same 'crime' ... five soldiers burst into her home, tied up her parents and took her away. She was found dead two days later, lying over a tree trunk with her hands tied behind her back. She was blindfolded and her mouth was full of rags. She had been raped and shot in the forehead.[20]

In spite of being victimized by warfare and violence, women's voices are seldom either raised or listened to. In a letter to the editor of the *International Herald Tribune* of 17 January 1992 concerning the civil war in Yugoslavia, Vanita Singh Mukerji of Tashkent, Uzbekistan, wrote that civilians who wanted no part of the war in Yugoslavia were not being heeded; she wished to share with readers the letter a Yugoslav friend had written to her which spoke poignantly of the human tragedy occasioned by the imbroglio and the masters of war:

What shall I tell my children? What shall I say to my Maria, born in Zagreb but living in Belgrade with her mother who is a Croat and her father who is a Montene-grin? What is she? How should she behave? Whom should she love, and whom hate?

I will teach her honestly and teach her that a person is a person, regardless of where he was born and where he lives. For me, the world was always without borders. That is why this creation of a tribal community on the threshold of the 21st century is incomprehensible to me.

I am desperate, in fear, in horror, in the expectation of something still more terrible. I am afraid for my children. I am afraid for their future. Who has the right to deprive them of their childhood? Who has the right to deprive them of a future? Who has the right to wage war in my name?

We are little people; we desire only our modest life. How many people have lost their lives, families, fathers, husbands, become homeless? How many lives of children have been wrecked? In the name of what?

## The uprooted

The most evident and numerous victims of war are refugees, and, according to the Office of the UN High Commissioner for Refugees (UNHCR), women and young girls now constitute the vast majority of the world's refugee population—at least 80 per cent. That population is growing rapidly. In 1970 the world refugee population stood at just under 2.5 million. By 1980 it had risen to 8.2 million. According to UNHCR there are today over 20 million refugees in the world, and a similar number displaced within the borders of their own countries.[21]

'Most of these refugees live in developing nations whose already fragile resources and infrastructure can barely sustain the needs of their own nationals', says Ann Brazeau, UNHCR's senior coordinator for refugee women. 'Many stay for prolonged periods in the country of first asylum before they can safely return home. Some may never return home and have little choice but to rebuild their lives in a new country ... Refugee movements must be seen as a critical factor in mainstream development planning rather than as peripheral to it. In the same way, inclusion of refugee women in such planning must be perceived as essential to efficient delivery of these programmes.'[22]

Women refugees bear the brunt of situations arising as a result of man-made violence, and are frequently victims twice over. In the first instance their search for protection and safety may be triggered by a situation involving violence as, for example, in war, civil disturbances and other forms of armed conflict, or by persecution as an individual because of political opinion, religious belief, or quite simply for refusing to accept the role that society seeks to impose upon them. Secondly, they may suffer violence during their flight, upon arrival in camps and settlements, and even in the process of being integrated into a new society, where they may find themselves in exploitative situations, entirely dependent upon others for the basic necessities of life.

'One of the most important phenomena with respect to the international protection of refugee women, and by far the most heinous one, involves the violation of their physical integrity and safety', says UNHCR. Indeed, refugee women face many complex and appalling obstacles to their security. In fleeing for their lives and those of their children they may be subjected to violations of their physical integrity and safety. The plight of the Vietnamese boat people is a case in point; several thousand refugee women, of all ages and usually with children, have suffered rape and abduction by pirates, frequently being passed among several boats to suffer inhuman abuses.

They had already given most if not all of whatever they possessed to get passage on a refugee boat, where conditions were a torture in themselves, and the chances of reaching the proposed destination were often slim. But falling prey to the pirates was the most cruel experience; any possessions left were taken, and they were either direct victims of rape or were forced to watch their children being raped: 'young girls, even children, who will bear the marks of this violence for the rest of their lives', says Meryem C. Anar.[23]

Susan Forbes Martin, in her book *Refugee Women*, quotes eye-witnesses of such pirate attacks:

Two of the young and pretty girls were taken to the front of the boat and raped. Everyone heard everything, all of the screams. That is what I remember, the screams. After a while the screams stopped, the crying stopped, and there was silence.

And again:

While all the men were confined to the hold of the refugee boat ... some if not all of approximately 15-20 women and young girls who were kept in the cabin of the boat were raped. The youngest ... was around 12 years old. Soon afterwards, the pirates set the boat on fire with all the Vietnamese on board. In the ensuing panic, the Vietnamese grabbed buoys, cans and floats and plunged into the sea. The crews of the pirate boats then used sticks to prevent them from clinging to floating objects ... Women and children were the first to perish.[24]

UNHCR says that there have been numerous instances elsewhere in the world where refugee women, in the course of their flight to safety, have been subjected to sexual abuse. A refugee woman interviewed in Djibouti described how, aged 18, she arrived from a two-week trek through the Danakil desert, physically exhausted, badly dehydrated, and with blistering sores from exposure on her feet and body. But the most terrible part of her ordeal was her three-day stay in the border jail, where she was raped repeatedly.[25]

Even after their arrival in refugee camps or settlements women may still continue to suffer such violations of their physical safety, including sexual exploitation, rape and prostitution. Abuse and abduction of refugee women by, for example, camp guards continue to be of great concern to UNHCR field officers, who report that it is also distressingly common for female refugees to fall victim to extortion and brutality both within and outside such camps and settlements:

> Pich Kola is 13 and from Indochina. She has been living in a refugee settlement for some three years. The camp is guarded but recently armed gangs from her country of origin have broken in to rob and terrorize the refugee population. Pich Kola's family hut is on the edge of the settlement so each night they move into the centre of the compound and sleep huddled together in the open.
>
> One night a gang entered the camp and went on a rampage which lasted for over five hours. Those refugees who could not pay the money demanded of them were simply killed by the attackers. Pich Kola hid in a fox hole. Her mother and sister were, however, not so fortunate: they were shot as they tried to flee.[26]

More fortunate refugees may make their way to new homes in strange lands where they will face problems of unemployment, cultural differences, language barriers and sometimes the hostility of the local population. Refugees often suffer profoundly from the psychological stress of the events which caused them to flee, compounded by the tribulations of their flight. When they are women with children and other dependents their sufferings are multiplied.

Distressingly large numbers of refugee women may, however, have to suffer even more. If they are among those confined for years to refugee camps, then to all of their burdens is added the hopelessness of being without freedom and facing an uncertain future for themselves and their children. Prolonged stays in closed refugee camps with no possibility of interaction with the local community raises the level of violence from which refugee women are the first to suffer. Thus, for some, there has been no escape. And the problems do not end there, says Angela Berry, UNHCR Nutrition expert:

> In an emergency, the health of refugees is put at risk by the lack of proper shelter and sanitary facilities ... Nearly a quarter of a million refugee children are suffering from acute malnutrition. Many more are struggling to survive on an inadequate and unbalanced diet. All are in danger of death and serious disease.[27]

Berry points out that over the past ten years an unprecedented number of cases and outbreaks of nutritional deficiency diseases have been documented in refugee camps. Hundreds of thousands of refugees, particularly in arid regions of Africa, have been affected, and the largest number has been within the traditionally vulnerable groups, women and children. In 1989, for example, reports of pellagra—a Vitamin B3 deficiency disease—were received from refugee situations in four southern African countries, the first time that this problem had arisen amongst refugee populations. 'The disease results from subsisting for more than two months on a "starvation diet" based primarily on maize. It is a very serious condition, leading to skin rashes, diarrhoea, mental illness and, eventually death.'[28]

Family life inevitably suffers when people are forced into exile. Parents become separated, from each other or from their children, and family roles change. Women may find themselves undertaking activities and assuming responsibilities which are new to them, while men have to come to terms with a change in their traditional status. In refugee camps, frustration and stress lead all too often to violence within the family, or between different tribes and clans expected to live in close proximity.

Wherever there is war or civil disturbance, there are refugees. And more than four-fifths of refugees are women and children. This fact alone should make women everywhere realize how important it is that they begin to influence local, national and world affairs in the direction of the peaceful resolution of conflict.

## Women under *apartheid*

Women and children under *apartheid* and other racist minority régimes suffer from direct inhumane practices such as massacres and detention, mass population removal, separation from families and immobilization in reservations. They are subjected to the detrimental implications of the labour migrant system pass laws and of relegation to the homeland, where they suffer disproportionately from poverty, poor health and illiteracy.[29]

This description in a United Nations document of *apartheid*'s effects on women summarizes most of the trials women must bear in an unequal and violent world. *Apartheid* is *institutional* violence, the very antithesis of economic and social justice. It is an intense example of a major premise of the Universal Declaration of Human Rights, 'if man is not to be compelled to have recourse, as a last resort, to rebellion against tyranny and oppression, that human rights should be protected by the rule of law' (Preamble).

Women under *apartheid* in South Africa have worked without protection of any of their rights as domestics or in the informal sector. As domestic servants they have had no legal rights, no minimum wage provision or minimum conditions of employment, no medical facilities, women's compensation or employment insurance. Some have been forced into prostitution, and have been subject to sexual harassment, conditions not unknown to millions of poor women.

Women have valiantly struggled against these conditions and have used all possible non-violent means open to them. In the South African townships they have been killed or injured. In the cities and elsewhere they have been jailed for their efforts at labour organizing, even though only 23 per cent of black women live in urban areas. Their entry into the cities has been restricted by pass laws when they migrate illegally, often to join husbands, from whom so many must endure long separations because Africans' low-paid labour is wanted in the townships.

The story of women's struggle against *apartheid* has been well illustrated by Hilda Bernstein in her book *For Their Triumphs and For Their Tears*.[30] The struggle has produced its heroines, among them Albertina Sisulu and Mary Moodley.

Jailed, kept in solitary confinement, banned, under house arrest and harassed in endless ways, they remained strong in their convictions as women struggling for freedom, justice and peace.

Although events in South Africa seemed recently to be moving painfully towards a solution, as Nelson Mandela and President de Klerk began to grope towards negotiation of a more just and humane society, government 'inability' to control police violence in the townships, and manipulation of the rivalry between Mandela's African National Congress (ANC) and the Inkatha Party, have cast a blight upon the negotiations.

Oliver Tambo, National Chairman of the ANC, speaking at a conference in Geneva in August 1992, pointed out that destabilization of black communities through surrogate mercenaries, and continued refusal of majority rule by a government trying to impose its power-sharing scheme, left the ANC with no alternative but to break away from negotiations. Mr Tambo had joined Yasser Arafat on the podium of a meeting of non-governmental organizations concerned with another example of *apartheid* and denial of human rights, that of the Palestinians in the Israeli-occupied territories.

## The Palestinians

As has been the case with black South African women, Palestinian women are victims of institutional violence. They have no vote, are discriminated against, are considered second-class citizens, and are harassed and at the mercy of the occupation authorities.

According to Amnesty, dozens of Palestinian women and girls have reported that Israeli interrogators have threatened them with rape and subjected them to sexually humiliating practices. One 70-year-old Palestinian woman was starting her pilgrimage to Mecca when she was detained at the Jordanian border, stripped naked and body searched, then held in solitary confinement at a police detention centre in Jerusalem. She was repeatedly beaten while interrogators made sexually explicit and humiliating remarks to her, and was later released without charge.[31]

The long years spent in refugee camps, and Israel's policy of building Jewish settlements in East Jerusalem and the occupied territories, have led to a violent uprising by young Palestinians (known as the *intifada*) in an attempt to win the right to an independent Palestinian state. Stone-throwing adolescents in the West Bank and Gaza have been killed and beaten by Israeli soldiers, and the army has maintained tough curfews, and closed schools and universities in reprisal. If soldiers suspect a Palestinian family of harbouring a stone-thrower, that family's house is destroyed, leaving the occupants homeless. On many occasions Palestinian families have been evicted from their homes in order that Jewish settlers could move in.

On 5 June 1992, the 25th anniversary of the Israeli occupation of the West Bank, Gaza and East Jerusalem, it was estimated by the United Nations that over 60 per cent of the West Bank and Gaza had already been confiscated. From the beginning of the *intifada* in December 1987 to March 1992 at least 1,032 Palestinians had been killed and over 121,000 injured by Israeli forces.

Conditions for the Palestinians, especially in the refugee camps of Gaza, are deplorable, although the Palestinians themselves are doing everything possible to improve their precarious existence. Palestinian women, as usual suffering more than most, have become steadily more active in attempts to relieve the worst effects of the occupation, although the Palestine Liberation Organization's (PLO) apparent support for Saddam Hussein during the Gulf War led to a dramatic drop in support, especially from other Arab States which were subsidizing the PLO.

Joint Israeli-Palestinian women's groups are doing what they can to influence the situation. An annual Women and Peace Conference takes place in Jerusalem each December, at which Women in Black groups report on their activities in North America, Europe and Australia. This important movement—similar to the Black Sash movement in South Africa—began in Jerusalem in January 1988 when a group of Jewish women decided to hold weekly vigils to protest against the occupation and the attendant violence.

Now hundreds of women stand in protest vigils in cities and towns throughout Israel every Friday between 1 and 2 pm. They dress in black to symbolize the tragedy of both the Israeli and the Palestinian peoples, and hold placards and banners calling for an end to the occupation. The movement has spread to cities in the United States and to London, Amsterdam, Rome, Milan, Turin, Venice, Bologna, Berlin, Munich, Aachen, and Zagreb. Another movement, the Women's Organization for Political

Prisoners, constitutes a kind of human rights watch by Palestinian and Israeli women who keep in close contact with prisoners' lawyers and families and support prisoners in their trial as observers in court.

This situation, a glaring example of the denial of human rights unworthy of a state which considers itself a democracy, may at last be moving towards a solution thanks to pressure upon Israel by the United States government and the election in June 1992 of a Labour government which declared its intention of pressing ahead with negotiations to give autonomy to Palestinians in the West Bank and Gaza as an interim measure. Jewish peace activists, and new Russian immigrants, can take much of the credit for the change in public opinion and the newly expressed desire for peace on the part of the Israeli people.

Peace talks with the Palestinians and with Jordan, Syria and Lebanon will nevertheless be extremely difficult, since the Labour Prime Minister, Yitzak Rabin, has also insisted that Israel will not leave the Golan Heights and East Jerusalem, or agree to an independent Palestinian state, which of course are the goals of their Arab interlocutors. The Israeli delegation's offer of limited administrative powers in the occupied territories, and its refusal to stop 'security' settlements or those already approved by the previous government, are unlikely to meet with an enthusiastic response from Palestinian negotiators.

A further danger for Palestinian women resides in the Muslim fundamentalism which is taking hold in Arab countries in the absence of an Arab/Israeli peace agreement. They risk sharing the experience of Algerian women who, when the Algerian Islamic Front (later outlawed) claimed that it had won elections in early 1992, saw the possibility of their hard-won freedom under a democratic government disappearing if fundamentalists were to achieve their aim of an Islamic society.

Curiously, a similar fate could lie in wait for women everywhere if Christian, Hindu, Judaic or other forms of fundamentalism continue their advance in erstwhile democratic societies, since a literal reading of the scriptures of all the main world religions appears to take the inferiority of women for granted.

## Protection of the vulnerable

In 1974 the United Nations Economic and Social Council's Recommendation to the General Assembly with regard to the protection of women and children in emergency and armed conflict reflected deep concern over the sufferings of women and children in the civilian population:

> All efforts shall be made by States involved in armed conflicts, military operations in foreign territories and in territories still under colonial domination to spare women and children from the ravages of war. All the necessary steps shall be taken to ensure the prohibition of measures such as persecution, torture, punitive measures, degrading treatment and violence, particularly against that part of the civilian population that consists of women and children ... All forms of repression and cruel and inhuman treatment of women and children, including imprisonment, torture, shooting, mass arrests, collective punishment, destruction of dwellings and forcible eviction, committed by belligerents in the course of military operations or in occupied territories shall be considered criminal.[32]

In the 17 years since that UN Recommendation was adopted, women and children have continued to be the overwhelming majority of civilian victims of armed conflicts all over the world. The 'repression and cruel and inhuman treatment of women and children, including imprisonment, torture, shooting, mass arrests, collective punishment, destruction of dwellings and forcible eviction' have continued to be committed by belligerents and in occupied territories, and their criminal nature implicitly condoned or ignored by the international community.

The UN Declaration on the Participation of Women in Promoting International Peace and Cooperation was adopted by the General Assembly at its 90th plenary meeting on 3 December 1982, Article 8 singling out women who are the victims of *apartheid* and racial discrimination:

> All appropriate measures shall be taken to render solidarity and support to those women who are victims of mass and flagrant violations of human rights such as *apartheid*, all

forms of racism, racial discrimination, colonialism, neo-colonialism, aggression, foreign occupation and domin-ation, and of all other violations of human rights.

UNICEF's *State of the World's Children 1992* calls war on children the 20th century's shame. Pointing out that, in the last decade, more than one and a half million children have been killed in wars and more than four million physically disabled through bombing, land-mines, firearms and torture, the docu-ment reports that there are five million children now in refugee camps and a further 12 million who have lost their homes, because of war:

This "war on children" is a 20th century invention. Only 5% of the casualties in the First World War were civilians. By the Second World War the proportion had risen to 50%. And, as the century ends, the civilian share is nor-mally about 80% — most of them women and children ... The time has now come for a worldwide public to cry out against this war on children — against those who use the weapons and those who supply them ... and insist that this appalling stain on the 20th century should not be allowed to seep over into the 21st.

In order to solve a problem, we must first understand it. If the slaughter of innocent civilians is to be prevented we must first look at the causes of conflict and hostility and see what can be done about them.

---

1    In *Non-Violence in Peace and War*, 1948.
2    Elise Boulding, 'Women and Peace Work', in *Women in the 20th Century World*. Sage, New York, 1977.
3    Reported in the *International Herald Tribune (IHT)*, 11/2/92.
4    Birgit Brock-Utne, *Educating for Peace*, Pergamon Press, 1985.
5    Elise Boulding, *The Underside of History*, p.684. Westview Press, USA, 1976.
6    Brock-Utne, op.cit.
7    Amnesty International Newsletter, *Women in the Front Line*, March 1991.
8    Amnesty International, *Focus*, London, March 1990. (Also Third World Network *Features*, Consumers' Association of Penang, Malaysia).

9     T.R.Reid and Robin Bulman, 'Korean Hostility Clouds Miyazawa Visit', *IHT*, 16/1/92.

10    Reported by David Singer, *IHT*, 8 July 1992.

11    Sister Mary Soledad Perpignan, 'The Militarisation of Societies and its Impact on Women', in *Women*, a publication of the Lutheran World Federation, July 1989.

12    Amnesty International, *Focus*, February 1992.

13    Ibid.

14    Ibid.

15    Most other examples are from Amnesty International's *Women in the Front Line*, March 1991.

16    From *One in Ten*, Rehabilitation International/UNICEF, New York. Vol.10, No.2-3, 1991.

17    Condensed from C.G. Cupie, 'One Woman's War Story from the Vukovar Front', *IHT*, 8/1/92.

18    Reported by Askold Kruschelnycky in *The European*, 3-6/9/92.

19    Amnesty International Newsletter, February 1992.

20    Amnesty International, op.cit.

21    Susan ForbesMartin, *Refugee Women*. Zed Books, London, 1992.

22    Introduction to *Refugee Women*, *o*p.cit.

23    Article in the UNHCR Magazine *Refugees*, June 1985.

24    *Refugee Women*, op.cit.

25    Ibid.

26    Ibid.

27    'Health in Exile', *Refugees* No.74, p.20. April 1990, UNHCR, Geneva.

28    Ibid. pp. 21-2.

29    United Nations Forward-looking Strategies, paragraph 259. Nairobi 1985.

30    Obtainable from the International Defence and Aid Fund for South Africa, London.

31    Amnesty International,*Women in the Front Line*, op.cit.

32    Doc. 1861 (LVI), 'Protection of women and children in emergency and armed conflict in the struggle for peace, self-determination, national liberation and independence'. 1897th plenary meeting, 16/5/74.

# 3. THE CAUSES OF CONFLICT

> It is but seldom that any one overt act pro-
> duces hostilities between two nations;
> there exists, more commonly, a previous
> jealousy and ill will, a predisposition to
> take offense.
>
> Washington Irving[1]

Why do conflicts erupt, and what can be done about them?
Many wars have erupted because of trade tensions, or because
of colonialism, or attempts to redraw frontiers. The *Economist*
believes that Yugoslavia's may well be the war of the future,
'one waged between different tribes, harbouring centuries-old
grudges about language, religion and territory, and provoking
bitterness for generations to come'.[2]

Ethnic conflicts often arise as the result of colonial powers'
arbitrarily drawn frontiers. Sometimes they are caused by the
influx of a new ethnic group which then competes for scarce
resources and benefits. While a growing population produces an
increased demand for resources, moving populations seeking to
meet their basic needs in the form of employment or food add to
social pressures and sometimes to political instability. Tensions
and conflicts often erupt in violence. As with other social crises
and human disasters, women bear the brunt of these pressures
and the resulting conflicts.

Ethnic and tribal strife, frontiers which divide peoples and
resources, military repression, political assassination, skewed
trading patterns, all of these are causes of warfare and civil disturbance. Another, of equal importance, is *structural* violence,
state expenditures on arms which lead to poverty and maldevelopment. One of the most important causes of conflict, in spite of
the end of the Cold War, is the threat in all parts of the world of
increasing emphasis on military values and ideologies.

## Militarism and militarization

In *Disarmament Prospects and Problems*[3] the World Council of
Churches has noted the following description of militarization
and militarism:

Militarization should be understood as the process where-by military values, ideology and pattern of behaviour achieve a dominating influence on the political, social, economic and external affairs of the state, and as a con-sequence the structural, ideological and behavioural patterns of both the society and the government are "militarized". Militarism should be seen as one of the more perturbing results of this process. Having said this, it must be noted that militarism is multi-dimensional and varied, with different manifestations in various circum-stances, dependent on historical background, national tradition, class structure, social conditions, economic strength, etc.

The report goes on to note the continuing spread and intensi-fication of militarization, cutting across rich and poor nations and ideological systems, and the fact that the root causes of mili-tarization remain unchanged. Among those root causes are the dominance of military concepts of security, competition between the major powers, the continuance of spheres of influence, the momentum of high technology, the arms trade, national security doctrines, and unstable political systems.The break-up of the Soviet Union at the end of 1991 has led to a considerable increase in the transfer of arms to the Third World, and to the heightened danger of nuclear proliferation.

It is clear that militarism is a major cause of world conflict. According to Ruth Leger Sivard, whose figures are recognized, and used, by the United Nations, during the 1980s global ex-penditures on arms and armies approached a trillion US dollars a year—US\$ 2 million a minute—and the number of wars escalated to an all-time peak. Three-quarters of the dead were civilians.[4]

As the 1990s began, things seemed to improve, beginning with the destruction of the Berlin Wall in November 1989 and the gradual disintegration of the Warsaw Pact. With the end of the Cold War the Soviet Union, the United States and 20 other countries signed in November 1990 the conventional arms reduction treaty, and conventional military forces based in central and eastern Europe began to shrink. The two super-powers collaborated in efforts to bring peace to Afghanistan, Angola and Cambodia, and covert support to Third World conflicts declined.

But, says Sivard, the various factors affecting national military programmes in 1990 had relatively little net effect on global military spending; the mild contraction in expenditures which began after a peak in 1987 shaved the *increase* over 1980 to about 20 per cent by 1990:

> This meant that estimated global military expenditures, after adjustment for inflation, were still more than 60 per cent above average annual outlays in the 1970s, and twice as high as in the 1960s. Other military indicators—armed forces, arms trade, nuclear inventories—remained at or near peak levels. Spending for military research began to drop in real terms, but continued to dominate government research priorities.

In fact, says Sivard, the world arms race continued at high speed in 1990, with preliminary data indicating that total military expenditures were about US$ 880 billion—adjusted for inflation, a dip of five per cent since the peak in 1987—and were among the largest military outlays on record:

> The world now has 26,000,000 people in the regular armed forces, another 40,000,000 in military reserves, a stockpile of 51,000 nuclear weapons, 66 countries in the business of peddling arms, 64 national governments under some form of military control, and 16 wars underway.

Sivard compares this with the mid-1930s, when, in reponse to the rise of Nazism in Germany, total global government outlays amounted annually to some US$ 4.5 billion—US$ 50-60 billion in today's prices—compared with close to US$ 900 billion a year spent annually by the world today. In the 1930s the US devoted one per cent of its GNP to military budgets, but now allots them over six per cent of its much larger GNP. Between 1960 and 1990, she says, 'total military expenditures (in constant 1987 dollars) amounted to two trillion dollars more than public expenditures for all levels of education, six trillion dollars more than expenditures for the health care of a rapidly growing, largely unserved, population.'

The extent of damage to human beings caused by militaristic policies is inestimable. Armed conflicts, investment in arms at the expense of health, education and social programmes and environmental damage have had lethal effects upon children and adults throughout the world. Women's groups have taken strong action to bring this question before the Earth Summit— the UN Conference on Environment and Development (UNCED)—which took place in Rio de Janeiro from 3-14 June 1992 (see Chapter 5, Arms and the Environment).[5]

When developing countries use scarce reserves for military purposes, badly needed social programmes are cut, leading to a marked increase in homelessness, hunger and suffering. 'Women have been disproportionately affected, for those who head families are four times as likely to be poor as male- or couple-headed families. Developing countries purchase military hardware on credit, using scarce foreign reserves and leaving mountains of debt for future generations.'[6]

## Weapons as status symbols

Unfortunately, as Sivard points out, weapons of mass destruction are seen by Third World countries as unchallenged status symbols of military power, as well as a practical means of discouraging attack. In spite of the tremendous investment of resources and time required, a few have tried the nuclear route, albeit secretly. India tested a nuclear device in 1974, and its neighbour Pakistan responded with an aggressive nuclear development programme. South Africa and Israel are thought to have collaborated in developing a small arsenal, and North Korea, Iran, Iraq and Taiwan are believed to be trying to do so. Argentina and Brazil suspended their secret programmes in 1990 and agreed to open their facilities to joint inspection.

But chemical weapons, offering less formidable technological problems than nuclear, have been the alternative choice for many developing countries, Sivard warns. They are apparently easier to acquire or produce and, although by no means as effective as nuclear bombs, can be powerful weapons of terror. While the use of chemical weapons is outlawed by international treaty, there is no prohibition as yet on production or possession. Meanwhile both the US and the former USSR have huge inventories of tens of thousands of tons, which they propose to reduce to 5,000 tons each by the year 2002. Israel is alleged to have stocks for offensive use and has a population protection programme, used as a defence measure during the Gulf War.

Biological weapons and ballistic missiles add other dimensions to the proliferation of unconventional weapons.

Meanwhile, international traffic in conventional arms is booming. Major arms exporters in the 20 years from 1969 to 1988, in cumulative billions of US dollars, included the USSR, the USA, France, UK, the Federal Republic of Germany, China, Czechoslovakia, Poland, Italy and Switzerland. Major arms importers during the same period included some of the poorest countries in the world.

---

### ARMING THE WORLD

| Major Arms Exporters 1969-88 billion dollars, cumulative | | Major Arms Importers 1969-88 billion dollars, cumulative | | | |
|---|---|---|---|---|---|
| USSR | 236 | Iraq | 61 | Afghan. | 10 |
| USA | 149 | S.Arabia | 37 | Algeria | 10 |
| France | 43 | Vietnam | 29 | Ethiopia | 9 |
| UK | 23 | Syria | 28 | Taiwan | 8 |
| West Germany | 18 | Libya | 27 | S.Korea | 8 |
| China | 15 | Iran | 26 | Turkey | 7 |
| Czechoslovakia | 14 | India | 22 | Jordan | 6 |
| Poland | 13 | Cuba | 16 | Greece | 6 |
| Italy | 11 | Egypt | 16 | Pakistan | 5 |
| Switzerland | 5 | Angola | 11 | S.Yemen | 5 |

Source: Sivard, *World Military and Social Expenditures 1991*
(figures rounded to nearest billion dollars)

---

One result of all this is the increasing power of the military, which have become increasingly influential on the political scene. Countries in which the military play a political role obviously tend to have high military expenditures per capita and a high ratio of armed forces to the population. They have also suffered more wars and an incredible number of deaths in wars, and tend to have a disturbing pattern of internal official violence. Many have used force and repression against the public, including torture, brutality, disappearances and political killings.

Sivard reveals that, in spite of their shocking record on human rights, none of the countries which frequently practised extreme forms of repression failed to receive a substantial flow of arms from substantive suppliers: between 1984 and 1988, 56 per cent of the arms delivered to the Third World went to countries with highly repressive governments.[7]

## Contributors to militarism

However, just as both women and men are victims of warfare and violence, so too both contribute to militarism. Women have supported their nations' military efforts in times of war by serving in non-combat roles in the armed forces, and were prominent in US forces during the Gulf War. Few women participate in the decisions to wage war, but without the contribution of women to the building and maintaining of war-making capacities war could not be waged. Indeed, many work in plants which produce parts for the most destructive weapons ever devised by man. Women are often intensely patriotic, accept that their sons and husbands go to the fighting forces, and feel that it is their duty to their country to support an operation which will decimate the population and destroy the very bases of civilized society.

Perhaps one of the most insidious ways in which women contribute to militarism is in the early education of their children. Militarism as a way of thinking and responding to problems begins at an early age, socialized into the behaviour of small children through their relationships in the home and violent messages in the media. Boys learn to resolve conflict through force, domination and control. Girls, taught that they belong to the weaker sex, learn the arts of compromise, accommodation and submission; later, as mothers, they continue to exhort their sons to 'be men', thus perpetuating a societal pattern of violence. Indeed, children in growing numbers are being used in armies and para-military forces, and a culture of violence is becoming deeply rooted in many societies.

Dr Elise Boulding has pointed out that women very rarely rear their sons to counteract militarism. 'A study of conscientious objectors in the United States during World War II showed that many of their mothers, particularly those outside the historic peace churches, opposed their taking the pacifist position.'[8] As

Boulding has noted, in one sense women prepare their sons for lifelong combat, whether in the occupational sphere, the civic arena, or the military battlefield.

One of the most pervasive, yet intangible, root causes of war can be found in the prevalence of family violence. If discord in the family is 'solved' by violence, whether it be by the husband against the wife, or by the mother against the children, there is little hope that it will not be seen as the only answer to problems on a larger scale. Those who suffered such family violence as children will inevitably believe that this is the only way to solve the situations which they will undoubtedly have to face as adults, and will automatically support solutions presented by their government which assume that only military measures can overcome national or societal difficulties.

Differences in attitude between men and women are primarily the consequence of socialization and learning, as are most forms of aggressive and violent behaviour. Women themselves, in accepting their roles as subordinates and victims, have contributed to the perpetuation of these attitudes, and thus to a violent world in which they are the first to suffer the consequences.

And yet, if the natural instinct of women is to nurture, to try to hold a family together, to settle disputes by conciliation rather than by aggressive measures, it is in giving these natural instincts full rein that women can help to change attitudes and raise a generation dedicated to the peaceful resolution of conflict. This aspect is further discussed in Chapter 8.

Many women peace activists believe that a zealously pursued process of demilitarization is an important factor in reducing both the direct violence of armed conflict arising from political and ideological struggles, and the indirect structural violence or economic exploitation caused by greed, competition and corruption. They are becoming a significant voice in confronting the major questions of peace, security and international cooperation.

But Scilla Elworthy has pointed out that 'the "serious" discourse on nuclear weapons worldwide, and all the decisions about nuclear weapons, are dominated by a tiny percentage of men who speak one particular language, peculiar to them, and see the problems in a particular and exclusive way. Out of 650 nuclear decision-making positions identified by the Oxford Research Group worldwide, only five are occupied by women.

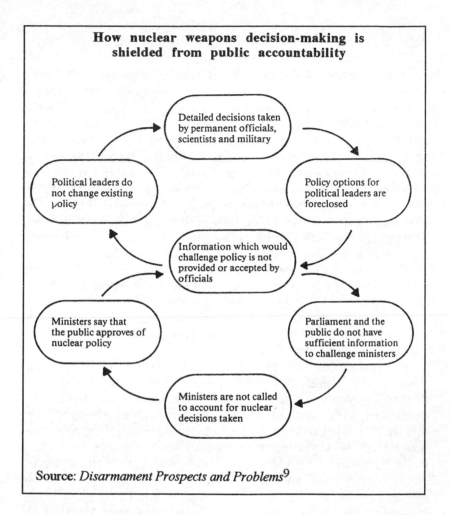

How nuclear weapons decision-making is shielded from public accountability

Detailed decisions taken by permanent officials, scientists and military

Political leaders do not change existing policy

Policy options for political leaders are foreclosed

Information which would challenge policy is not provided or accepted by officials

Ministers say that the public approves of nuclear policy

Parliament and the public do not have sufficient information to challenge ministers

Ministers are not called to account for nuclear decisions taken

Source: *Disarmament Prospects and Problems*[9]

99.9% of adult citizens of the world are systematically disempowered by three factors: concentration of power in non-elected hands, secrecy, and the arcane jargon of the experts.' Elworthy's diagram of the situation shows how nuclear weapons decision-making is shielded from public accountability.[10]

As we have seen, women and children are not only the worst victims of wars and of militarization, they are also left out of the decision-making process in terms of defence strategies and expenditures in all parts of the world. Chapter 7 discusses further the role of women in decision-making.

## The violence of maldevelopment

Maldevelopment—the division of the world into rich and poor countries, and the gap between rich and poor within those countries—is a potent force for the eruption of violence. Today, thanks to high military expenditures and to the international debt crisis of the 1980s, more than a billion people cannot meet their basic human needs. It is estimated that four-fifths of the human race are trying to survive on one-fifth of the global resources, while the remaining one-fifth of humanity consumes four-fifths of those resources. World population, at present 5.5 billion, is expected to rise to about nine billion over the next four decades. Most of that growth will be in the cities of developing countries, leading to a massive increase in poverty and squalor.

Throughout the world, social and economic structures and processes, from local to global level, are serious obstacles to a decent quality of life and to the full development of the individual. That is to say that the poverty which condemns millions to hunger, disease, illiteracy, unemployment and alienation is, in fact, a powerful form of violence.

In Zambia, for example, child deaths caused by malnutrition more than doubled in the 1980s, according to Allan Thompson of Gemini News Service. He quotes OXFAM to the effect that, in most of Africa and much of Latin America, average incomes fell by 10-25 per cent over the past decade. While the cause has much to do with plummeting commodity prices and restrictive trade practices, OXFAM also points to root causes in the developing world itself, including lack of democracy and multiple military conflicts; annual military spending in developing countries shot up by an average of 7.5 per cent over the past 25 years.[11]

The United Nations has estimated that, if the Third World were to simply freeze military spending, US$ 15 billion could be released for investment in human development and the promotion of democratic pluralism. 'In South Asia and sub-Saharan Africa, where the needs are greatest, some governments are spending two to three times as much for weapons as for education and health. Yet that is where most of the world's billion absolutely poor and illiterate live and where 180 million malnourished children can be found, of whom 3 million die in childhood from preventable diseases.'[12] The United Nations Development Programme (UNDP) has estimated that Third World arms expenditure in relation to GNP is outpacing that of the West by a 3-to-1 margin.

Families suffering the stress of poverty, unemployment, illness, malnourished and untended children, cannot provide a strong social base or bring up a generation of healthy, socially responsible youth. Households often solely supported by women have to absorb and fulfill needs and health services that society should but cannot provide, adding to family stress and the burden of women. Cities with inadequate public transportation and communications systems, plagued by unemployment and homelessness, cannot be centres of commerce and production on which healthy economies can be based. And perhaps no other long-range cost of arms expenditures will so affect the future quality of life as the lack of resources for education—a crucial factor in social, cultural and economic development.

According to Sivard, the world's military expenditures had already reached US$ 900 billion at the time of the International Year of Peace, 1986, an amount later outstripped as annual expenditure on arms rose to US$ 1,000 billion, or more than the total Third World debt. Although, six years later, the Cold War is over and military expenditures are slightly lower, they remain at record levels, contrasting with the slowdown in world economic growth.

## A silent genocide

Dr Bernard Lown and Dr Eugene Chazov, co-founders of the International Physicians for the Prevention of Nuclear War (IPPNW) have said that one in eight people worldwide lives in a state of destitution so total that it constitutes 'silent genocide':

> Over one billion people, one-quarter of the world's population, are seriously ill or malnourished. In regions of Southeast Asia, nearly 40 per cent of the population is afflicted with malaria, measles, diarrheal and respiratory diseases as well as hunger. In sub-Saharan Africa ...10 million children die every year of causes which are easily and inexpensively preventable ...

Large pockets of abysmal poverty and want exist among the mighty superpowers. In the US about 15 per cent of the people lack any health insurance; 315 million have no roof over their heads; 20 million people go hungry several times a month. Yet over the past decade the US has invested almost 3 trillion dollars in the military, or $45,500 for each US family.

The military investments of the USSR have been equally enormous, the economic and social situation incomparably grimmer. Both superpowers have behaved like moral pygmies, providing abundance for mighty military machines and crumbs for the needs of their own people.[13]

Former US Secretary of Defense Robert McNamara and his colleague Nicole Ball have suggested that aid to developing countries by the International Monetary Fund (IMF) be tied to reductions in defence budgets. A number of countries are already adopting this approach to bilateral aid; Germany has said that it will cut aid to India by nearly 25 per cent in 1992 unless New Delhi reduces its military budget, and Pakistan and China are expected to receive similar warnings. Japan has told North Korea that to obtain diplomatic recognition and aid it must halt construction of the Yongbyon plutonium plant. It is now suggested that the IMF should make economic and technical assistance contingent on these and similar policies.[14] The other side of the equation is, of course, that the industrialized countries must stop *selling* arms to developing countries.

The word 'peace' can mean the prevention of armed conflict and military occupation, intervention by one country in another, or the use or threat of force in dealing with international, national or local problems, but it can also refer to cooperative relationships between nations which recognize the importance of trust and mutual respect and see the Earth as a single, interdependent system, with one common future.

This interpretation assumes that all peoples have the same fundamental human needs and are entitled to the realization of all human rights, and that they share a common interest in the future of the planet. It presupposes a social environment characterized at every level, from local to global, by tolerance, mutual respect, and serious attempts to understand and respect differences and to build understanding and confidence so that conflicts of all kinds can be resolved without recourse to violence.

The United Nations is dedicated to the achievement of a peaceful world through the exercise of diplomacy and the resolution of conflict by peaceful means. In no instance have the promises of the United Nations Charter been so betrayed as in the 1991 Gulf War.

---

1    In 'English Writers on America', *The Sketch Book of Geoffrey Crayon, Gent*, 1819-20.

2    *The Economist*, 21/12/91-3/1/92, p.73.

3    Commission of the Churches on International Affairs, *Disarmament Prospects and Problems*. Background Information, 1990/2, World Council of Churches, Geneva.

4    Ruth Leger Sivard, *World Military and Social Expenditures 1991*. World Priorities Inc., Box 25140, Washington DC 20007, USA.

5    Official Report, World Women's Congress for a Healthy Planet, Miami, 8-12 November 1991. WEDO, 845 Third Avenue, New York, NY 10022.

6    Paper produced by the Lutheran World Federation for the International Consultation for Women in Mexico City, 28/8-7/9/89.

7    Ibid.

8    Elise Boulding, extract from 'Women and Peace Work', *Women in the 20th Century World*.

9    Op.cit.

10    Scilla Elworthy, 'Decision-making on Defence—An Overview', in *Disarmament Prospects and Problems*, op.cit.

11    As reported in UNICEF quarterly *First Call for Children* No.1, March/April 1992.

12    Editorial in the *IHT*, 29/5/91.

13    In a foreword to *World Military and Social Expenditures 1989*.

14    In an article, 'Make aid conditional on demilitarization', in the *IHT*, 13/1/92.

# 4. LESSONS OF THE GULF WAR

> **There never was a good war
> or a bad peace**
> Benjamin Franklin[1]

In January 1991, under the leadership of the United States and with the blessing of the United Nations, a consortium of nations declared war on Iraq, which had invaded Kuwait some months earlier. At the time of the invasion, the UN invoked sanctions upon Iraq in order to induce it to withdraw, but these were given little time to show their effectiveness. Prolonged and difficult attempts by the USSR, France, King Hussein of Jordan and the United Nations to negotiate a peaceful solution to the crisis were brushed aside with the decision to go to war, and within only three months of the vote to apply sanctions devastation rained down upon the Iraqi people, under relentless bombardment by the most barbarous weapons ever devised. It seems to have been deliberate policy to destroy all economic, physical and social life in Iraq with the most destructive and inhuman weapons ever deployed.[2]

## A United Nations war?

The war waged upon Iraq by the US and its allies in the name of the United Nations, following its invasion of Kuwait, can in no way be considered a 'United Nations war'. It led to huge loss of life, massive dislocation of peoples, separation of families, loss of land and livelihoods, exile for many, a rapid deterioration in the quality of life, and environmental catastrophe. The number of civilian casualties—referred to by the Pentagon and the media as 'collateral damage'—was immense, as was the impact on hospitals, health-care services, schools and the entire infrastructure. It is estimated that some 100,000-150,000 Iraqi soldiers were killed—sons and husbands of grieving women who were themselves under bombardment.

It was reported in February 1992 that a new Defense Department study had come to the conclusion that much heavier damage was done to Iraq's civilian infrastructure than had been intended, especially with regard to its electrical generating facilities. Huge damage to power plants resulted in the long-term shutdown of sewage treatment and water purification plants and the hampering of medical services.[3]

Among the victims were thousands of infants whose deaths, far in excess of the normal rate, could be attributed to the shortage of infant milk formulae and medicines. This, according to former US Attorney General Ramsey Clark, who travelled around Iraq in early February 1991, was largely due to the fact that an infant and baby milk processing facility in Baghdad was an early target of US bombing; the US claim that it manufactured chemical warfare material was later proved false.[4] The impact of this upon Iraqi women, their own lives at risk, seeing their homes destroyed and their babies dying for lack of milk and medicine in circumstances over which they had no control, does not need a great effort of imagination.

The US government did not consider Congressional approval necessary for the declaration of war, or for its lead role in this UN action. Because of its military might, and its determination to protect its oil supplies, the United States was able to persuade a coalition of thirty-seven governments, including those of Saudi Arabia, Egypt and other Arab states, to take joint action to repel the aggressor. Indeed, US Congressman Henry Gonzalez (Texas) accused the President of bribing, intimidating and threatening members of the UN Security Council in return for their votes in support of war against Iraq:

> The debt of Egypt was forgiven; a $140 million loan to China was agreed to; the Soviet Union was promised $7 billion in aid; Colombia was promised assistance to its armed forces; Zaire was promised military assistance and partial forgiveness of its debt; Saudi Arabia was promised $12 billion in arms; Yemen was threatened with the termination of support; and the US finally paid off $187 million of its debt to the UN after the vote President Bush sought was made. The vote was bought, and it will be paid for with the lives of poor and minority soldiers ... and thousands of innocent civilians.[5]

Many voices, in the US and elsewhere, were raised in protest against the way in which the UN was used for this act of international violence. Stephen Lewis, Canadian Ambassador to the UN from October 1984 to August 1988, considered that 'the United Nations served as an imprimatur of legitimacy for a policy that the United States wanted to follow and either persuaded or coerced everybody else to support. The Security Council thus played fast and loose with the provisions of the UN Charter. For instance, sanctions were invoked under Article 41, but there was never any assessment of whether those sanctions were working or might work sufficiently before the decision was made to resort to force under Article 42. Moreoever, no use was made of the Military Staff Committee, which under Article 47 is supposed to direct any armed forces at the Security Council's disposal.'

Ambassador Lewis did not think this was the UN's finest hour. 'In some respects, in fact, it may have been the UN's most desolate hour. It certainly unnerved a lot of developing countries, which were privately outraged by what was going on but felt utterly impotent to do anything—a demonstration of the enormous power of US influence and diplomacy when it is unleashed ... I think the whole war was a catastrophic mistake; I never saw a shred of justification in it. And I think it's heartbreaking that the United Nations should be conscripted into the role of providing cover for US foreign policy.'6

Many shared Ambassador Lewis's distress and alarm. Peace vigils and demonstrations were held by women's groups around the world, and in Paris women presented a petition to the President of France protesting against the war and demanding a referendum on their country's involvement. In Spain demonstrators demanded the shut-down of military bases in the country used as staging points for US troops in the Gulf;  some 3,500 people walked 14 kilometres from Madrid to the air base at Torrejon de Ardoz and a similar number to the naval base at Rota.

In Japan 1,000 demonstrators formed a human chain near a US Navy base in Sasebo, while in Tokyo 1,500 attended a rally that focused on environmental damage caused by the war. Some 20,000 protesters marched through central London, while in Italy about 3,000 protested at Camp Darby, a US army base near Pisa. In Australia Marta Romer, speaking for Jewish Women in Support of an Independent Palestine, insisted in the *Sydney Morning Herald* that 'we must, as Jews, voice our opposition to the Israeli military presence in the occupied territories and to the war in the Persian Gulf'.

Groups such as the Women's International League for Peace and Freedom (WILPF), Women for Mutual Security (WMS) and the Women's International Democratic Federation (WIDF) protested both internationally and at the national level through their many members worldwide. These three groups organized a meeting in Geneva 2-3 February 1991, presided by Margarita Papandreou, Global Network Coordinator for Women for Mutual Security and former wife of a President of Greece. Seventy-five angry women came from 26 countries—including Iraq, the United States, Egypt, Israel and the occupied territories, Tunisia, Greece and Britain—to demand an immediate cessation of the war and to discuss ways in which women could influence the situation. They unanimously decided to wear black and white armbands (symbolizing grieving and hope for peace) until the war was over, and to wear black on International Women's Day, 8 March.

They urged women to demonstrate and hold regular vigils, organize broad anti-war coalitions, work with the media, visit foreign ministries, participate in a worldwide plebiscite on peace, devote one hour a day to anti-war activities and boycott products related to arms industries. The meeting's resolution to the United Nations expressed horror at the suffering of peoples in the region, the destruction of the environment, the cost of the war, the harm to relations between peoples, religious and ethnic groups, and the damage that war under the auspices of the UN had done to its image as a peace-keeping and peace-seeking organization. The UN was requested to set in motion the holding of an international conference to resolve all conflicts in the Middle East, and for UN treatment of the Iraq/Kuwait conflict to be taken to the International Court of Justice for an advisory opinion.[7]

In fact, protests brought millions of people into the street all over the world, and a massive anti-war movement took shape before the war even began. The groundswell was reminscent of the intensity of protest reached toward the end of the war in Vietnam. To give but one example, two days before the 15 January deadline set by the United Nations, Israeli WILPF members participated in a Human Chain for Peace, organized by Peace Now, the Union of Arab Mayors and others, in which some 20,000 Israelis and Palestinians joined hands along a 15-mile stretch of highway in central Israel. Such demonstrations were reported by the media in many countries, thus encouraging others to join the movement.[8]

## US aid to Iraq

Ironically, it was largely due to aid from the United States during the Iran-Iraq war that Saddam Hussein was able to launch his attack on Kuwait. According to Seymour Hersh in a report published in the *New York Times* in January 1992,[9] facts have now emerged which show that the Reagan Administration secretly decided to provide highly classified intelligence to Iraq in the spring of 1982. It also permitted the sale of American-made weapons to Baghdad, allowing Israel to ship American arms and spare parts valued at several billion dollars. US officials have acknowledged that American arms, technology and intelligence helped Iraq avert defeat and eventually grow, with much help later from the then-Soviet Union, into the regional power that invaded Kuwait in August 1990, thus sparking the Gulf War.

As early as in 1983, American arms dealers such as Lebanese-born Sarkis Soghanalian, based in Miami, began selling Iraq sophisticated Soviet arms purchased in Eastern Europe; although this was known to the Central Intelligence Agency (CIA), the Agency did not interfere. Officials say that satellite imagery, communications intercepts and CIA assessments were forwarded to Iraqi commanders to show them 'where the Iranian weaknesses were', and top-secret intelligence was supplied to Iraq by the US until the Iran-Iraq war ended in 1988.

Nor did the US government intervene when American-made arms flowed into Baghdad from Iraq's Middle East allies, even though US export law forbids the third-party transfer of American-made arms without Washington's permission. Jordan and Saudi Arabia sent Iraq American small arms and mortars, among other weapons, and Kuwait sold the Iraqis thousands of American anti-tank missiles. Even the mobile launchers used by Iraq to fire dozens of Scud missiles at Israel and Saudi Arabia are said to have been made for Iraq by an American company and their export condoned by the CIA.

This in spite of the fact that, shortly after taking office in 1981, the Reagan Administration had allowed the Israelis, bitter foes of Saddam Hussein, to ship American arms valued at several billion dollars to Iran. According to a former senior State Department official, the decision to help Iraq was not a 'CIA rogue initiative'—the policy had been researched at the State Department and approved at the highest levels. 'We wanted to avoid victory by both sides', he said.[10]

## The origins of the dispute

The events leading to Iraq's invasion of Kuwait in August 1991, politically complex, were due to a number of factors, including three grave miscalculations on the part of the protagonists. Put simply, overproduction of oil by Kuwait had forced the price of oil far below the target set by the Organization of Petroleum Exporting Countries (OPEC), thus lowering Iraq's oil income and reducing the funds available for reconstruction of the damage caused by the Iran-Iraq war. At the same time, Iraq accused Kuwait of slant-drilling oil from wells in Iraq's Rumaila fields, across the frontier. Strategic rivalry was also building up, due to Iraq's desire to build a naval facility on its Gulf coastline which required control of the two small, uninhabited islands of Bubiyan and Warba for its security. Moreover, Kuwait was insisting upon repayment, with interest, of loans made to Iraq during the Iran/Iraq War, which Iraq had assumed would be forgiven on the ground that it had saved Kuwait from invasion by Iran.

Negotiations between the two countries had been under way for months, but finally broke down. According to Milton Viorst, in an article in *The New Yorker*, the Kuwaitis are said to have taken a very hard line and adopted an arrogant tone in the negotiations, feeling secure in American support promised during recent visits by US General Schwarzkopf. They offered no concessions on oil production limits, control of the islands or possession of the Rumaila oil fields, and were seemingly unaware that Iraq, its position desperate, was deadly serious.[11] This was the first grave miscalculation.

Although Iraq's original intention may have been to seize only the small islands which blocked its access to the Gulf and the oil terminals through which the Iraqi oil was being drawn, the disastrous decision was made to invade the whole of Kuwait. This was the second grave miscalculation, this time on the part of Saddam Hussein, and the Iraqi people and many others would pay dearly for it.

Poorer Arab nations had long been appalled at the conspicuously high consumption level of the Kuwaitis in a region of great poverty and underdevelopment, especially since the Islamic religion clearly indicates that the rich must share their wealth with the poor. In spite of announcing that Kuwait would become the nineteenth province of Iraq, the invading army sacked the country and systematically destroyed it. Resistance suspects were arrested, tortured, taken home for a brief reunion with their families, and then shot and left on the sidewalk. A good number of them were women.[12]

The invasion by Iraq of its neighbour Kuwait was an unpardonable and unacceptable act of aggression. The sanctions against Iraq mandated by the Security Council were supported and approved by the entire international community, and were surprisingly free of violation by UN member states. As in the case of sanctions applied elsewhere, for example against South Africa, the pressure they would exert on the miscreant would only become apparent over a period of time, as they began to cause shortages and problems in Iraq. They were, however, overtaken by the events which precipitated full-scale war.

**Whose oil?**

Concerned that the whole of Middle East oil would fall into the hands of someone they considered a dictator, who could then blackmail consumer nations, the US reacted with all the strength of its considerable might. And the third grave miscalculation was that of the American government, which insisted that the US would on no account negotiate with President Hussein.

Negotiation—bargaining—is an integral part of Arab culture, and it is a rare deal in that part of the world which is reached without long, courteous talks in which both sides take considerable pleasure. To insist that Iraq accept American terms without negotiation was, therefore, a deadly insult, making it impossible for Saddam Hussein to retreat. In effect, President Bush painted both Saddam and himself into a corner from which there was no egress without the use of military power.

There were many, including in the US government, who wished to give negotiation and sanctions a chance, but a US president derided for months as an incoherent 'wimp', and wishing to show that he could be tough, decided that force must be used without delay, and Iraq was attacked with the most deadly air assault on record. The opportunity was taken to test the latest in high-tech weapons and aircraft, and the result was a military victory within six weeks and a huge and unmitigated human disaster.

Hailing it as a 'clean' war, because there was a relatively light loss of their own military lives, the allies glossed over the thousands of Iraqi dead and injured, the terrible devastation of their country, and the floods of refugees and displaced persons, the majority of them women and children. Strict measures were applied on both sides to control media reports on the war, so that news of the real situation only became known to the public considerably later, although those able to receive CNN, the cable news network, saw some of the devastation at first hand.

## The social and economic costs

Quite apart from the military costs of the war (US$ 61 billion, of which US$ 7 billion was paid by the US and the rest by its allies around the world)[13]—funds thereby denied to development—there were the inevitable social and economic costs to society, including the deaths or incapacitation of at least 50,000 civilians (by some estimates, more than 100,000) and the loss by foreign workers of hundreds of thousands of jobs in Kuwait.

This led to huge streams of refugees who fled to Jordan, and the loss of the wage remittances which the workers had been sending home to their families in Pakistan, Bangladesh, and other countries. The largest core of foreign workers, the Palestinians, were deported by the Kuwaitis to Jordan, and were not allowed to return because of PLO support for Saddam Hussein. The Jordanian economy suffered a heavy blow in the attempt to give succour to all these refugees, an attempt in which many women's organizations took the initiative, the YWCA prominent among them.

The war led to a precipitous drop in international travel, trade and tourism, and considerable damage to the environment caused by pollution from the burning of over 500 oil wells in Kuwait, where reconstruction was estimated to cost US$ 70 billion. The rise in oil prices brought inflation in its train. Rehabilitation in Iraq is expected to cost some US$ 200 billion but has been delayed because UN sanctions (on all goods other than medicines and some food) remain in place—a measure insisted upon by the US and its allies unless and until Saddam Hussein relinquishes his presidency of Iraq. Meanwhile Saddam Hussein, still in the seat of power, has achieved something approaching martyr status in the Arab world.

Great dismay has been expressed in many countries, and among UN staff, that Security Council Resolution 678 was contrary to the spirit and purpose of the United Nations, and the UN may find, in spite of its impressive peace-keeping achievements elsewhere, that the legitimation of the Gulf War by the international organization whose founding mission was 'to save succeeding generations from the scourge of war' has tarnished its reputation. The 'success' of the Gulf War has already become a question mark in the light of its catastrophic aftermath in terms of destruction and widespread recession.

Ironically, it would seem that the world went to war in 1991 against an Arab country which, for all its faults, had made more progress than most in the region in terms of social and economic development, in order to save one of the most autocratic, undemocratic régimes in the Arab world. But then, the official US line was that America's war aim in Kuwait was legitimacy, not democracy.

Basic health and sanitation standards in Iraq deteriorated precipitately, power supplies were cut, medicine was in short supply, and rising prices made it difficult for women to buy food for their families. The situation of children, no longer being inoculated against dangerous diseases, became particularly serious. There was rising malnutrition and an increase in crime. Thousands of homeless Kurds fled to camps in northern Iraq or to Iran, where thousands of Shiite refugees, who left during the revolts against Saddam Hussein following the Gulf War, had also found refuge. Iraq's oil wealth will be mortgaged for years to come to meet the billions of dollars it will take to repair its infrastructure and to pay UN-mandated compensation and reparations to Kuwait, Iran and other countries, not to mention its enormous foreign debt.

At the same time, according to the UN Conference on Trade and Development (UNCTAD), the Gulf War deeply affected the economies of the least-developed countries (LDC). Financial shortfalls due to reduced flows of private remittances from nationals previously employed in the Gulf region, the crisis in the tourism industry, reduced export earnings on account of slower growth in the economy of their trading partners, higher import costs of capital goods and manufactures, and reduced aid flows formerly originating in countries of the Gulf region, all dealt a heavy blow to the economies of the LDCs.[14]

For example, the losses incurred by Bangladesh as a result of the Gulf conflict have been estimated at US$ 1,400 million, including loss of workers' remittances, loss of export earnings, loss of belongings, savings and salaries of Bangladeshi employees in Iraq and Kuwait, and the cost of repatriation and initial rehabilitation of returning nationals. Jordan, among those most affected, faced a dramatic decline in its *per capita* income profile as it attempted to cope with a huge refugee influx.

Yemen faced a similar situation, a million Yemenis—the equivalent of about eight per cent of its population—having been forcibly returned from Saudi Arabia and Kuwait, an influx threatening the newly unified country's fragile political and economic stability. The loss in workers' remittances was estimated at about US$ 400 million. In addition, the Aden oil refinery is thought to have lost about US$ 40 million in 1990 and US$ 220 million in 1991 as a result of the loss of oil shipments from Iraq and Kuwait, and faced the loss of about US$ 554 million provided by these two countries in the form of budgetary support, project financing and concessional lending. Export earnings shortfalls due to loss of exports to these same countries were estimated at US$ 43 million in 1990 and US$ 52 million in 1991.

In all, the shortfalls in private transfers from migrants working abroad, together with higher imports, added US$ 2,300 million to the combined current account deficit of the LDCs in 1990.[15]

## The victims

Whether Iraqi women under bombardment or displaced from their shattered homes, trying to feed and care for their families amid the devastation of the war, Kurdish women fleeing into the mountains with their children, Kuwaiti women under Iraqi attack, Asian and Palestinian women trying to keep their families alive in refugee camps in Jordan, or Palestinian women suffering under curfew in the occupied territories, the major victims of the Gulf War were there for all to see.  Many lost their lives when the vehicles in which they were fleeing from Baghdad to Amman came under direct Allied bombing attacks.

A graphic description of the human cost was given by Paul McGeough in the 31 January 1991 edition of the *Sydney Morning Herald*. Pointing out that the military rarely gave details of what they euphemistically called 'collateral damage', he said that detail was left to the refugees:

> They are not brilliant on figures, but they know a roasted corpse when they see one; they know a cratered highway when they have to detour into the scrub; they know hunger when they see friends eat cats and dogs; they know cold when only a blanket lies between them and the wind-driven snow; they know loneliness when a friend dies in the desert chill. They are now coming across the Iraq-Jordan border traumatised, sick and stripped of dignity and possessions.

McGeough quotes a high-school teacher who told him that all the children who made the journey were sick. 'In all, we know of two children and three women who died from no food in the cold and rain.'

Those perennial victims, the Palestinians, were particularly affected by the Gulf War, partly due to the PLO's support for Iraq. As Viorst points out: 'It was hard to make the case to Kuwaitis that the PLO was reacting not against Kuwait but against America's long-standing support of Israel and indifference to the Palestinian cause.' Before the war Kuwaitis made up less than a third of the country's population. Among the rest, the foreigners who did the real work of the society, Palestinians numbering 400,000 were the largest group. Although many of these had been residents for decades, half were forced to leave during the war; by August 1991, fewer than a hundred thousand remained, and these were gradually being expelled and replaced by Asian labour. [16]

The needs of those Palestinians who stayed in Kuwait during the occupation were ignored; they were subjected to abduction as alleged collaborators, and to house-to-house searches. 'Dozens of Palestinians were beaten and hospitalized, and scores—one government official said that the toll might actually be as high as a thousand—were summarily executed.'[17] Those charged as collaborators were forced to leave the country without trial and driven in buses, hundreds at a time, to the Iraqi border and dumped on the other side where, having no country of their own to return to, and forbidden by Israel to go to the occupied territories, they became stateless refugees.

Among them, of course, were a large number of women who had escaped the refugee camps in the occupied territories with their families and had worked hard to make a life of their own in their new country. Now they would have the same status as those Palestinian women who had been refugees for more than 40 years, their suffering immeasurably increased by *apartheid* conditions under the Israeli occupation of the West Bank and Gaza Strip.

Even in the occupied territories the Palestinians were penalized during the Gulf War. They did not receive the gas masks distributed to all Israeli citizens. The government clamped a day-and-night curfew on the West Bank and Gaza for ten weeks, confining the entire population of 1.7 million Palestinians to their homes. Although food supplies were distributed by the United Nations Relief and Works Agency (UNRWA), on some occasions food brought to refugee camps could not be delivered because the Israeli authorities refused to lift the curfew to allow camp residents to receive them. This was in violation of a prior agreement between the Agency and the Israeli authorities under which UNRWA would be permitted to distribute foodstuffs donated in response to a worldwide appeal for assistance to the Palestinians.[18]

Inevitably, the confinement imposed physical suffering and psychological strain on refugee families, especially those living in the crowded refugee camps of Gaza. And no one felt the strain more than the women, trying to look after fractious children at home and find food for the family.[19] For Amneh, living with 13 other family members in two small rooms in a crowded refugee camp, the curfew that fell every night at 5 pm meant an unbearable struggle with noise and tension, and fear that doctors could not be reached were a child to fall ill. During the *intifada* years virtually no town in the territories has escaped curfews, and there are few Palestinians who do not tell of being fined for infractions, of being routinely questioned by soldiers, of being dealt with coarsely, of being beaten.[20]

The improvements in living conditions for women and children in the Gulf region which had been accomplished since the end of the Iran/Iraq war and the unification of Yemen were wiped out by the Gulf action, according to UNICEF. In Iraq basic health and sanitation standards deteriorated to critical levels, and devaluation of local currencies eroded the purchasing power of local populations, severely affecting women's capacity to buy food. Only a lifting of the trade embargo could relieve a population suffering under the impact of punitive economic sanctions. [21]

Amnesty International reported a serious increase in attacks on human rights in many countries as a result of the Gulf War, including the arrest or imprisonment of many people with dissident views about the crisis. They included Magdy Ahmed Hussein, an Egyptian journalist and deputy leader of the Socialist Labour Party who spoke against the war at a Cairo mosque, while in Turkey three Socialist Party members were arrested for opposition to the war. An American soldier was jailed in the US because he refused to help prepare supplies for troops in Saudi Arabia, and thus became a 'prisoner of conscience'. [22] In Australia there were personal attacks on immigrants of Arab origin.

In wartime the risk of arbitrary detention escalates, people are detained without charge or trial, with no possibility of defending themselves against the authorities' accusations.  A leading Palestinian advocate of a peaceful solution of conflicts in the region, Dr Sari Nusseibeh, was arrested by Israel and put in administrative detention, while Abe Nathan, a leading Israeli proponent of a peaceful settlement of the Palestinian question, has been jailed several times by his own government. Dr Hanan Ashrawi, one of the leaders of the Palestinian delegation to the Middle East peace talks, has been constantly at risk of imprisonment by the Israelis or assassination by those who oppose the peace negotiations.

## Democracy in Kuwait and in Saudi Arabia

One slim hope entertained by the allies was that Kuwait, where women have no vote and are considered second-class citizens, would keep its commitment to become more democratic and emancipate its women and long-time residents. Saudi Arabia, too, had indicated that it would become a more democratic state.

Alas, it would seem that neither country is moving in that direction, although Viorst reports that Kuwaitis, who like to think of themselves as modern, 'have grown increasingly uncomfortable at having to make excuses for [the ruler's] practice, technically authorized by the Koran, of marrying and divorcing young girls—perhaps dozens of them, in rapid succession ... Observers of the royal family estimate that Sheikh Jabir has fathered at least seventy children.'23

'The war wasn't fought about democracy in Kuwait. The war was fought about aggression against Kuwait', said President Bush in July 1991 when questioned about Kuwait's atrocities against Palestinians and other foreign residents after the Iraqis had been defeated. The expulsion of thousands of Palestinian and stateless Arabs who had been allowed to live all their lives in Kuwait brought condemnation from neither the United States nor the United Nations.

It is still against the law for more than five persons to meet, if they plan to issue a public statement, without permission from the government, and it is still the case that only male descendants of male Kuwaitis who were counted in a 1920s census may vote. The quasi-democratically elected National Assembly has been suspended since 1986. Parliamentary elections would have to lead to far-reaching reforms if the basic human rights of all residents are to be recognized and respected.

Although Saudi Arabia has formed a Consultative Council (Majlis Ashoura), and made other administrative changes intended to give Saudi citizens a forum in which to debate the country's policies, there has been no mention of elections, so that real democracy in Saudi Arabia is not likely to be on the horizon. The Council consists of at least 70 members, selected by the government from among the country's academic, business and religious élite, to review new laws, foreign and domestic policy initiatives and give its views to the king.

It is considered highly unlikely that women will ever be among the chosen ones. Saudi Arabian women, who dismissed their chauffeurs and drove their own cars in a one-day demonstration during the Gulf War, in an effort to force reform after watching American army women driving jeeps and enjoying equal status with their male colleagues, were swiftly returned to the back seat and look as though they will have to stay there.

## A hollow victory

Many lessons can be learned from this 'Nintendo' war. Among them are that active negotiations must continue until conciliation is arrived at; that UN sanctions against a country which has invaded another, once applied, must be given a chance to work; that any use of force for 'the maintenance of international peace and security' must be on the basis of the advice of a reactivated United Nations Military Staff Committee; that the greatest number of casualties in the wars of today are civilians; and that the use of force does not lead to desired results—the basic problems with regard to rich and poor oil-producing countries, and the Israeli-Palestinian conflict, remain unresolved. If Saddam Hussein is still president of his country, and still seen in some quarters as the champion of the Arab world, it is because of the immense frustration engendered in that region by its recent history of injustice, poverty and malde-velopment. Iraq remains a military power, and Iran is in the process of a multibillion-dollar arms build-up.

Failure to prevent the war in the Gulf and to solve the region's problems peacefully resulted in an orgy of destruction, disruption and distress. The people of the world, mired in recession, will be paying the bill for decades to come. Perhaps the only ones to have benefited are the oil companies, whose profits soared during the Gulf crisis, the banks to which capital flowing out of the Gulf region came for safe keeping, and above all the arms manufacturers, who were happy to see so many of their high-tech weapons being tested in some real action. But, as usual, it was a case, in the words of John Kenneth Galbraith, of 'the poor killing the poor'; most of the armed forces charged with the killing were from the poorest segments of US society.[24]

In order to put the Gulf War into a perspective more easily understood in the Arab world it is important to remember that, while sanctions were speedily applied to Iraq, no sanctions have ever been applied in response to Israel's annexation of the Golan Heights, its long military occupation of East Jerusalem, the West Bank and Gaza, and the constant invasions of Southern Lebanon which, to the Arab world, it seems able to carry out time and time again with total impunity in spite of condemnations by the UN Security Council. In February 1992, smashing through United Nations barricades and seriously wounding two UN peace-keepers, an Israeli armoured force took its revenge on Palestinian attacks on Israelis by invading, yet again, southern Lebanon, killing Sheikh Abbas Musawi, a Shiite leader, his wife and child, and totally destroying two Lebanese villages. In fact, according to Israeli officials, the decision to eliminate Sheikh Musawi had been taken months before.

The Gulf War aroused expectations among Arabs that solutions to the Palestinian and other issues would be agreed to or imposed upon the parties concerned. Subsequently, pressure has been applied by the United States to bring Israel and the Arab States to the conference table, and the election in June 1992 of a Labour government in Israel may hasten the peace process.

Failure of these negotiations to arrive at a just solution, including mutual recognition of Israel and of an independent Palestinian state, will be exploited by extremist movements taking advantage of the dangerously explosive mixture of population increase, large-scale unemployment, growth of the refugee population, and immense frustration. It is estimated that some 60-70 per cent of the Arab population in the Middle East is under 20—ripe territory for that violence which is the voice of the voiceless.

## The No-Fly Zone

The application of 'double standards' became even more apparent in late August 1992. At a time when immediate action was being urged to prevent further killing and destruction in Bosnia-Herzogovina, the United States, the United Kingdom and France instead imposed a flight exclusion zone in southern Iraq in order to 'protect Shiite rebels'—a muscular move which coincided with polls showing President Bush's weak position in the US presidential elections. Iraq was warned that all military aircraft in the 'no-fly' zone must be grounded, or would be shot down by Allied aircraft overflying the region.

The action was considered by most commentators to be not only unwise but illegal, and not mandated by the United Nations. Although UN resolution 688, which required Iraq to halt oppression and authorized continued monitoring of human rights, was cited by the United States, that resolution concerned the imposition of a flight exclusion zone to protect Kurdish refugees in the North, who were crossing international borders and becoming a threat to peace; it did not invoke Chapter 7 of the UN Charter, the legal basis for armed enforcement.

Indeed, the action aroused great fear in States bordering Iraq. Already the protection measures imposed in Northern Iraq had enabled the Kurds to hold legislative elections with a view to establishing a separate state, a development watched closely by Iran, Turkey and Syria, which have sizeable Kurdish minorities on their borders, all of them susceptible to agitation for a new, enlarged and independent Kurdistan.

If, under Western protection, the Shiites in Iraq follow the Kurdish example, tensions between Sunni and Shiite Muslims in the whole region would be exacerbated, Saudi Arabia would feel threatened, and Iraq would be reduced to the middle third of its territory—a landlocked area deprived of most of its oil and at the mercy of Iran, which supports the Shiites. Although Iraq invited UN anger by obstructing inspection procedures— American inspectors were included in the teams and were even, in one instance, in charge—and by its refusal to abide by UN resolutions, it is not surprising in the circumstances that Iraq considered its sovereignty to have been violated, and saw the 'no-fly zone' as an attempt to overturn what was still its legitimate government. Nevertheless, that government proposed defusing the confrontation with the West by establishing a 'wise men committee'—an offer which was immediately refused.

By their action the Allies ran the risk of a confrontation with Iraq and of further military action, causing yet more suffering for the civilian population of that country. Beyond that, they risked destabilizing the entire Middle East and increasing the chances of its domination by fundamentalist Iran.

---

1    In a letter to Josiah Quincy, 11/9/1773.

2    International law prohibits the use of all indiscriminate weapons, including those that cause unnecessary suffering or superfluous injury. These include the Rockeye cluster bombs and exploding dum dum bullets used by US forces in the Gulf War.

3    Michael R. Gordon, in the *International Herald Tribune*, 24/2/92.

4    Ramsey Clark, 'How Iraq was decimated', in *Third World Resurgence*, March 1991. Article based on a letter to the UN Secretary-General, 12/2/91.

5    Extract from a letter from US Congressman Henry Gonzalez (Texas) to peace activist Sissy Farenthold, 23/1/90, published in *Pax et*

*libertas*, Vol.56, No.1, March 1991. Women's International League for Peace and Freedom, Geneva.

6    Jim Wurst, interviewing Stephen Lewis in 'A Promise Betrayed'. *World Policy Journal*, Summer 1991.

7    *Pax et libertas*, op. cit.

8    Ibid.

9    Reprinted in the *IHT*, 27/1/92.

10    Ibid.

11    Milton Viorst, 'After the Liberation', *The New Yorker*, 30/9/91.

12    Ibid.

13    Figures given by Eric Schmitt in the *IHT*, 16/1/92.

14    The group of LDCs currently comprises 42 countries, with a combined population of nearly 440 million.

15    UNCTAD, Doc. TAD/INF/2160, 14/3/91.

16    Milton Viorst, op.cit.

17    Ibid.

18    UNRWA, *Palestine Refugees Today*, No.129, April 1991.

19    Ibid.

20    As reported by Clyde Haberman, 'For West Bank town, curfew is a nightly grind', *IHT*, 29/1/92.

21    Heather Jarvis, speaking at an international conference on 'Winning the Peace' organized by the Gulf Crisis Working Group in London, 29/5-1/6/91.

22    Amnesty International note on 'Human Rights in the Shadow of War', February 1991.

23    Ibid.

24    John Kenneth Galbraith, 'Poor vs. poor, war after war', in *Development Forum*, United Nations, March-April 1991.

# 5. WHAT CONSTITUTES SECURITY?

**Our small planet is getting endangered: by the arsenals of weapons which could blow it up; by the burden of military expenditures which could sink it under; and by the unmet basic needs of two-thirds of its population which subsists on less than one-third of its resources. We belong to a near universal constituency which believes that we are borrowing this Earth from our children as much as we have inherited it from our forefathers. The carrying capacity of Earth is not infinite, nor are its resources. The needs of national security are legitimate and must be met. But must we stand by as helpless witnesses of a drift towards greater insecurity at higher cost?[1]**

A concept of national security which gives priority to military threat rather than to dangers in the economic and social sectors of society can be bought only at the cost of poverty and misery and the violation of human rights—a cost borne by all poor people but especially by women and future generations. According to the United Nations, security 'consists of not only military but also political, economic, social, humanitarian and human rights and ecological aspects. Enhanced security can, on the one hand, create conditions conducive to disarmament and, on the other, provide the enforcement and confidence for the successful pursuit of development.'[2]

John Kenneth Galbraith, the noted American economist, has pointed out that poor countries 'collectively spend a larger percentage of their gross national product on arms than do the rich; they import weapons in the range of $30 billion a year ... The consequence is enormous cost to the poorest of the world's people ... the mirror image of present military expenditure in the poor lands is civilian deprivation, starvation and death.'[3] It is an explosive situation, which can only lead to greater violence unless funds at present devoted to the arid, sterile needs of a 'defence' which no longer provides security can be diverted to the educational, health and development needs, and indeed the survival needs, of the poor, and especially to the most vulnerable among them, the women and children.

The Final Document of the UN Special Session on Disarmament drew attention to the danger in 1978:

> The hundreds of billions of dollars spent annually on the manufacture or improvement of weapons are in sombre and dramatic contrast to the war and poverty in which two-thirds of the world's population live. This colossal waste of resources is even more serious in that it diverts to military purposes not only material but also technical and human resources which are urgently needed for development in all countries, particularly in the developing countries.[4]

It is only too true that excessive expenditures on defence and militarization have reduced the amount of funds available for the measures which, by overcoming poverty and underdevelopment and the mistreatment of the environment, constitute the only real security in the world of today. In spite of technological advances, the world continues to be a world of rich and poor. Population continues to explode, Third World health and education needs continue to be neglected, and ecological mismanagement threatens the survival of the human race. The so-called 'peace dividend' which was supposed to result from the end of the Cold War, liberating funds for development purposes, seems to be disappearing or being swallowed up in the aftermath of the break-up of the ex-USSR and the formation of newly independent states of Eastern Europe, now themselves in need of considerable aid.

**Arms and the environment**

Although the impact of military production and activity on the global environment has received scant public attention, one major women's group, the Women's International League for Peace and Freedom (WILPF), points to emerging evidence which suggests that global military activity may be the most serious, if not the largest, worldwide polluter and consumer of precious resources. Its impact on the environment is both direct and indirect, both real and potential, beginning with the mining and diversion of the earth's resources and continuing step-by-step through the manufacturing, testing and deployment of weaponry to peacetime military exercises and, finally, to war, of which one example, the Gulf War, led to devastating environmental damage over the entire Middle East, caused by the burning of over 500 oil wells in Kuwait:

> The environmental costs incurred throughout the military production cycle are compounded by the enormous risks posed to the environment from accidents or wars, and by the lost opportunities resulting from the annual diversion of an estimated US$ 1,000 billion in global resources for military purposes. These squandered resources represent the indirect but nonetheless real costs of the military to the environment ... if invested in the environmental and developmental sectors, these resources could go a long way in arresting environmental degradation and in environmental clean-up and protection.[5]

The US National Oceanographic and Atmospheric Administration (NOAA) has estimated that 175 million barrels of oil were spilled onto the sands of Kuwait. Some oil lakes were more than 1.6 kilometres long and nine metres deep. Oil known to have been released from damaged supertankers and oil facilities totalled 5.5 million barrels, compared with the 250,000 barrels of crude spilled by the *Exxon Valdez* in Alaska. Millions of grebes, plovers, flamingos, cormorants and terns migrating north from North Africa and the southern Gulf never arrived, and some species, such as the Socotra cormorant, could face extinction as a result of the Gulf War.

Iran claims that half the trees and crops in its western province were destroyed by acidic fallout from the oil fires. The effect on human health was equally serious.[6] Reconstruction in Kuwait, it was estimated, would cost US$ 70 billion, money which could have been devoted to the essential development and environmental needs of the region.

A comparison of the costs shows that sums transferred from military expenditure could be applied to global environmental problems to great effect. Ruth Leger Sivard has provided an environmental budget which would amount to just over a third of the cost of the National Aeronautics and Space Administration's (NASA) space station. She points out that tropical forests are disappearing at the rate of 13 to 20 million hectares per year, affecting the lives of one-fifth of humanity. One-third

## An Environmental Budget

| Development | Cost in US$ | Defence |
|---|---|---|
| Reforest the earth | 2 billion | Nuclear submarine |
| Provide safe water | 5 billion | More nuclear bombs |
| Roll back the desert | 2 billion | A dozen nuclear tests |
| Protect the ozone layer | 1 billion | More space flights |
| Reduce air pollution | 5 billion | 6 nuclear bombers |
| Conserve natural assets | 4 billion | Arms for Middle East |
| Stabilize population | 6 billion | More arms for the ME |
| Clean up hazardous wastes | 10 billion | Still more arms for the Middle East |
| More environmental research | 10 billion | Down-payment on NASA's $120 billion space station |

Source: *World Military and Social Expenditures 1991.*
(US$ 1 billion = US$ 1,000 million.)

of the world's people has access only to impure water, which is a contributing cause of 80 per cent of Third World diseases. Ninety per cent of the 90 million people added to the world population each year live in the developing countries, where urban pollution fosters the spread of typhoid fever, cholera and hepatitis, while overcrowding in the industrialized world leads to high levels of energy use, foul air, water and soil.

The violation of a human being's right to economic and social security is considered to be a form of structural violence. It is compounded by the fact that poverty is induced and increased by high governmental expenditures on weapons, and by the arms trade.

The debt crisis of the 1980s was partly caused by Third World expenditure on armaments, for in spite of their desperate need for development Third World countries as a group spent 23 per cent more of their resources on foreign weapons between 1978 and 1988 than they received in economic development aid. And this in spite of the fact that interest payments on Third World debt exceeded the amount of aid received from the developed countries, i.e. more funds were leaving the country in interest payments than were coming in under foreign aid programmes. The result has been a disturbing increase in real poverty, with its impact, as always, first and foremost on women.

Questions concerning the nature of real security have, for women's action networks, assumed increasing importance and have been the subject of a number of important conferences, among them the World Women's Congress for a Healthy Planet, held in Miami 8-12 November 1991 in preparation for the Earth Summit, the United Nations Conference on Environment and Development (UNCED) held 3-14 June 1992 in Rio de Janeiro.

The brainchild of Bella Abzug, former US Congresswoman and co-chair of the Women's Foreign Policy Council, the Congress was convened by the Women's International Policy Action Committee (IPAC) and the Women's Environment and Development Organization (WEDO) and attended by 1,500 women from 83 countries, ranging from full-time activists, agronomists and bankers to nurses, parliamentarians, technicians and zoologists. They came from UN agencies, governments, non-governmental organizations and grassroots groups, universities, foundations and the news media.

Women from every region of the world presented dramatic evidence of their battles against ecological and economic devastation before a tribunal of five eminent women judges. From this testimony they developed Women's Action Agenda 21, for presentation to the Conference. While not included as such in the Plan of Action adopted by UNCED, the Agenda will continue to serve as a blueprint for incorporating the women's dimension into local, national and international environment and development decision-making.

The Agenda's recommendations included a strong statement on Women, Militarism and the Environment which declared that military expenditures, the arms trade and armed conflict deprive billions of human beings of basic security and well-being and that all military activity, including research, development, production of weaponry, testing manoeuvres, presence of military bases, disposal of toxic materials, transport and resource use, has a disastrous environmental impact, often leading to occupation of lands and the denial of human and environmental rights.

The declaration called for all nuclear weapons to be dismantled and destroyed, for the complete cessation of nuclear testing, space activities and supersonic flights which threaten the ozone layer or release carbon dioxide, and a 50 per cent reduction in military spending. It also proposed creation of national civilian commissions, with half the members women, to open to public scrutiny all military activities, expenditures and research and development; that national armies be converted into environmental protection corps, and that daughters and sons be educated to shun military service if military power be used to exploit the resources and peoples of other nations.[7]

The Second International Women's Conference on Security and Cooperation in Europe (WCSCE-II) is another example of women's increased concern with questions of security. Held in Brussels on International Women's Day, March 1992, it was organized by Women in the New Europe and the NATO Alert Network, and attended by many prominent pacifist women, including Margarita Papandreou.

## Economic conversion

One of the most significant contributions in the whole field of disarmament— a United Nations Expert Report on the subject of economic conversion—was prepared in 1982 by a commission chaired by Inge Thorsson, then Swedish Secretary of State for Disarmament, and became known as 'the Thorsson Report'. It made a strong case for the link between disarmament and development, demonstrating the negative economic and social effects of arms spending on both industrial and developing countries. This Report gave considerable impetus to enquiry into the possibilities and consequences of economic conversion from military production to goods and services which would meet human and social needs and accelerate the development process.[8]

Although the causes of underdevelopment are varied and complex, and military spending accounts for only one of them, economic conversion has become an issue of great concern and interest to researchers, international organizations and peace activists. If savings from disarmament are in fact going to be channelled into development, much research and planning will be required. Several experimental programmes have already been launched and a large number of studies, particularly on effects on employment, have been undertaken.[9]

Between 1961 and 1990 the US Defense Department put almost 100 former military bases to civilian reuse. The Pentagon says that more than 93,000 jobs at the bases were lost, but more than 158,000 were created for civilian airlines, air freight companies, industrial parks, educational establishments and other civilian uses. Today, switching from military to civilian production is complicated in the United States by the comfortable relationship between defence contractors and the government, by high unemployment and by economic recession.

But savings from defence reductions could help to finance conversion, with tax credits on new investment. Private facilities can also be converted; the owner of a small Colorado manufacturer of defence-aircraft seating has successfully started making specialized cabin-crew seating for commercial jets.[10] Thousands of high-technology jobs in Colorado Springs, which thrived on billions of dollars of military contracts in the 1980s, are now switching to the civilian sector to work with Apple Computer and MCI Telecommunications. The shift to civilian work has been slower at aerospace companies, but Lockheed Missiles and Space Co. in Sunnyvale, California, which built six generations of navy missiles, is now producing designs for Motorola's Iridium system of 77 satellites to relay signals from pocket phones around the globe.

Seymour Melman, chairman of the US National Commission for Economic Conversion and Disarmament, believes that economic conversion is crucial to creating a full-employment, productive US economy, but that it is essential for this to be planned in advance, and at both national and local levels. Such planning would involve selecting new products, evaluating their market, retraining employees and redesigning production methods and plant facilities. Bases could be converted to industrial parks, schools, hospitals, airports and recreational facilities, while military laboratories could perform invaluable work in meeting society's technological needs such as preventing pollution and the search for renewable energy resources. Many of the products now imported by the US, such as machine tools, electric locomotives, farm machinery, oilfield equipment and consumer electronics, could be produced by converted factories.[11]

Transfer of resources from the military to the civilian sector would reap many social and economic benefits for all people, in particular for women. Many of the current gross inequities in education, health and employment could be redressed, at least at a starting level. Women's health needs in particular would be better served by biological and scientific research concerned with such objectives as the development of nutrition supplements and safe methods of family planning, rather than with research in connection with chemical and other forms of warfare.

Construction of housing, schools, and health care centres in place of bombers and aircraft carriers would better serve the health and well-being of the whole society. Such conversion would require education and training for less-costly civilian sector production to meet long-range social and consumer needs—more open to women than military production, which uses female labour mainly for certain forms of difficult, precision handwork and usually on an exploitative basis.

Plans for conversion to civilian purposes are taking shape in the ex-Soviet Union. For example, a group of small manufacturers of tableware in Tsubame, near the Japan Sea port of Niigata, is exploring the idea of converting Siberian weapons plants into production sites, turning missile parts into forks and spoons. Japanese tourism developers plan to use the port of Vladivostok, which has long been home to the Soviet Pacific fleet, and a Niigata sweater maker is sending yarn and test patterns to a workshop in the port. The Korean Hyundai conglomerate invested in a Siberian logging joint venture in 1990 and is now building a 200-room hotel in Vladivostok.[12]

Many of Sivard's WMSE reports spell out in detail what specific benefits in terms of public health and social welfare could be gained by the reduction of military expenditures. Thousands could be housed for the cost of a bomber, or could be educated for the cost of a missile. Since 1955 the US government has spent more than US$ 1 trillion on research and development of nuclear arms and other weaponry—62 per cent of all federal research expenditures, according to the National Science Foundation. Today, industry has surpassed the federal government as the nation's prime patron of science research.[13]

But in spite of general agreement that technology turned to the enhancement rather than the destruction of life would clearly make for a more humane society, economic considerations can lead societies to turn in the wrong direction. In late February 1992 Fred Hiatt of the *Washington Post Service* reported that Russia had decided that it must actively promote arms sales overseas at the expense of converting weapons factories to civilian purposes.

Senior Russian officials have indicated that Russia's dire need of hard currency, and the dismal state of its vast military-industrial complex, meant that conversion, although remaining a prime focus of government policy, was losing ground to those who believed that Russia could quickly reap billions of dollars by selling tanks, fighter jets and other weapons abroad. Air Marshall Yevgeni I. Shaposhnikov, commander-in-chief of the joint armed forces of the Commonwealth of Independent States, has argued that, with profits from arms sales, Russia could buy equipment to produce the consumer goods the country so desperately needs. Such sales would, of course, only increase the danger of arms proliferation (see Chapter 1).[14]

It should be borne in mind that economic conversion, while vitally important, would be only one component of several interrelated processes and structural changes directed towards strengthening international peace and security. In addition to being geared to disarmament and development, it would have to be accompanied by confidence-building measures, effective dispute settlement procedures, and proposals for international peace-keeping. However, in itself economic conversion would be a major step toward that goal.

## Disarmament and development

The international community has agreed that 'Peace, security, and economic and social development are indivisible.'[15] So when the claim is made that there are vital relationships between disarmament, development and security, it must be understood that such security is the fuller and broader authentic security which cannot be achieved without a massive reallocation of resources from arms to development, from preparing for war to preparing for peace.

This deep and significant relationship led the United Nations to call an International Conference on the Relationship between Disarmament and Development in 1987—a Conference the United States did not attend. Its purposes included 'consideration of the implications of the level and magnitude of military expenditures ... for the world economy and the inter-national economic and social situation, particularly for the

developing countries, and formulation of appropriate recommendations for remedial measures'; and 'consideration of ways
and means of releasing additional resources, through disarmament measures, for development purposes, in particular for the
benefit of developing countries.'[16]

In the Conference's Final Document, participating governments expressed their determination to adopt, both individually
and collectively, appropriate measures to implement commit-
ments in the fields of disarmament and development, and
stressed the importance of respect for international humanitarian
law applicable in armed conflicts. They recognized the need to
give practical expression to the relationship between disarmament and development through specific measures at national,
regional and global levels, and reaffirmed the international
commitment to allocate a portion of the resources released
through disarmament for purposes of socio-economic development, with a view to bridging the economic gap between developed and developing countries.

They also agreed to consider keeping under review issues
related to conversion from military to civilian production,
undertaking studies and planning for that purpose as well as to
identify and publicize the benefits that could be derived from the
reallocation of military resources. The results of experience in,
and preparations for, solving the problems of conversion in their
respective countries would be made available to other countries.

The Final Document also recognized that an informed public,
including non-governmental organizations, had an invaluable
role to play in promoting the objectives of disarmament and
development and in creating awareness of the relationship
between disarmament, development and security. The United
Nations and the Specialized Agencies were requested to give
increased emphasis in their disarmament-related public information and education activities to this perspective and to make
greater efforts to promote collective knowledge of the non-
military threats to international security.

It has been well-documented in recent research on development and arms spending that women bear the greatest burden of
the world's poverty and are more vulnerable in situations where
basic needs are unsatisfied and which might be more adequately
provided for were not so large a portion of the world's
resources spent on war and preparation for war. This linkage is
acknowledged by more and more of those women who are

becoming politically aware and active promoters of world peace. They link their demands for peace with very concrete social demands, for equality, development and the solution of global problems.

Such women were among the main organizers of the Non-Governmental Organizations' (NGO) Conference on the Relationship between Disarmament and Development held in Stockholm in May 1987 in preparation for the Special UN Conference. The NGO Statement pointed out that 'more than three billion of the world's people, even after three United Nations Development Decades, have insufficient access to the means of a dignified human life. There are more poor in the world than there were thirty years ago. The gap between the poor and the rich is widening, not narrowing. The debt burden of the South hits the trillion dollar mark. This is major evidence of the negative flow of wealth from the poor to the rich. Millions die every year, from hunger, malnutrition and the lack of simple medical care.'[17]

The Statement welcomed all workable proposals to reduce global military expenditure and to devote resources so saved to programmes to meet genuine human needs:

The bottleneck in development has not been just lack of funds; the real problem in development is an unjust political and economic structure which warps all development ... the development issue should be reformulated to correct mistaken, paternalistic and misleading notions of development which are divorced from the reality of political and economic structures within and among nations ...

There is no alternative to disarmament, general and complete, as a final goal. There is also no alternative to a just and participatory development. But both have to find their fulfilment in a new international political-economic, social-cultural and humanitarian-moral order in which our common security will be based on mutual trust and cooperation rather than on weapons and mistrust. For no peoples or nations can regard themselves as free and secure as long as others are oppressed, exploited or insecure.[18]

The concept of *partnership* has been embraced by women's groups, as evidenced by the meeting in Crete 4-11 October 1992 organized by Margarita Papandreou's Women for Mutual Security under the title: The First International Minoan Celebration of Partnership—The Right of Survival. The need for a 'new-mindedness' (attitudinal change), and the enlargement of survival chances of millions who, through no fault of their own, are condemned to die by war, poverty, hunger, hatred, destruction and pollution of their natural habitat, is leading women to look for ways in which they can make a greater contribution to the building of a partnership society where equity, ethics, justice and human-centred values are key, and to develop the means and methods whereby people can turn some of the pages of history themselves.

## The 'peace dividend'

The need for governments to agree to 'allocate a portion of the resources released through disarmament for purposes of socio-economic development'[19] was echoed at a North-South Round-table held in Costa Rica in January 1990 on 'The Economics of Peace', at which the chair pointed out that it would cost only $2-3,000 million a year—one day's global military expenditure—to tackle the readily preventable causes of child mortality world-wide and thereby reduce by half the 14 million under-fives dying unnecessarily each year.  What was needed was:

A global bargain which uses the peace dividend from reduced military spending to ensure greater human development in both developed and developing countries, to find a satisfactory solution to the current debt crisis of the Third World, to divert more resources to protect the global commons, to obtain concrete agreements for nuclear non-proliferation and to ensure a future of economic and social justice. An international framework for a peace dividend, which should be linked to local, national and regional plans for the retraining of military personnel, the destruction of military equipment, and the conversion of arms industries to peaceful uses.[20]

The problem is that the Western world is in deep recession, and industrialized country governments have a great belief in the recession-curing powers of government spending, especially on arms. In an article in the *International Herald Tribune* of 29 May 1990 Bernard Nossiter pointed out that nearly every postwar president since Harry Truman had fought recession, at least in part, with an increase or speed-up in arms spending. 'Thus Dwight Eisenhower, despite his farewell warning against the military-industrial complex, twice used arms as a counter-cyclical device in 1954 and 1958 ... John Kennedy then ended Ike's last slump with nearly $6 billion in space and arms spending. [But] the great military Keynesian, of course, was Ronald Reagan. He enlarged Pentagon purchases of goods and services by $70 billion in three years to end the deepest slump since the Great Depression.  Given this history, George Bush is understandably reluctant to depress the economy with genuine military cuts or abandon a tool so useful to his predecessors.'

Nossiter's conclusion is that, although a slump can be offset by expanded outlays for health, housing, schools and more, these are politically entangled, arousing philosophical and business opposition. 'That is why it is unlikely that budgets at the Pentagon, an important tool of economic management, will suffer much shrinkage in the years ahead. There is even less chance of trimming them until the facts of the postwar experience are discussed more openly.'

The following day, 30 May 1990, the *International Herald Tribune* published an article by Robert Pear of the *New York Times* reporting that, 'Because of unexpected increases in food prices in the last eight months, at least half the American states have moved to cut government food allotments for poor women and children or to stop the aid altogether for thousands of these people. Among those being deprived of the food in some states are children who have inadequate diets but who do not yet show clinical signs of malnutrition.'

Michel Camdessus, Managing Director of the International Monetary Fund, has emphasized the necessity to curtail 'unproductive spending', including that on the military, in order to meet the need for global savings and investment in the years ahead. He has pointed out that, if all countries decided to reduce their military spending to the level of the worldwide average of 4.5 per cent of gross domestic product recorded in 1988, annual worldwide savings of 14 billion dollars (14,000 millions) would be generated.

And even Edward Teller, who helped the United States develop the hydrogen bomb, has pleaded that the 'peace dividend' be used directly to help the Russians, in much the same way as, after World War II, the US contributed to the recovery of its former enemies, Germany and Japan. 'Russian accomplishments in space technology could be utilized for the benefit of mankind, for example, constructing better instruments of observation that could turn meteorology into a real science and furnish a sound basis for the measures that need to be taken against worldwide pollution.'[21]

Although charts could be drawn up to show how small transfers from military budgets could meet great human and social needs, what must be considered are the long-term implications, not only for the people—particularly the children—whose needs go unfulfilled, but for the society and the economy itself. The 'investment' of scarce and vital resources into the military has had an extremely destructive effect on social infrastructures, productive capacity, the environment and the quality of life.

## European 'security clubs'

There are five bodies in Europe which have 'something to do' with security: the Conference on Security and Cooperation in Europe (CSCE), the Council of Europe (C of E), the North Atlantic Assembly (NAA), the North Atlantic Treaty Organization (NATO), and the Western European Union (WEU). All will to more or less extent be involved in rethinking the concept of security in a continent where the threat of violent Cold War confrontation has disappeared, including the question of troop reductions and their impact on European countries both east and west. The end of the Cold War has called the role of NATO into question and led to discussion of a 'new security architecture' for Europe based on the CSCE, which has thus acquired a new importance.

The CSCE, founded in 1975 and grouping close to 50 nations (European and ex-Soviet Union, plus USA and Canada) was set up to foster East-West contacts in three areas: security, human rights and trade. In 1990 it established a parliamentary assembly, a small secretariat in Prague, a conflict-prevention centre in Vienna, and an elections office in Warsaw. Its influence is likely to grow, especially in view of decisions taken at the July 1992 meeting in Helsinki, giving it a stronger role, in collaboration with NATO and the WEU, in dealing with the crisis in the Balkans. Its job has also been enlarged to include giving early warning of potential conflicts, improving crisis management, and developing military confidence-building mechanisms so as to avert tensions among the newly independent states of the ex-USSR.

The C of E, in Strasbourg, has a Convention for the Protection of Human Rights and Fundamental Freedoms and a human rights commission and court which can declare governments in breach of their obligations. It also deals with health, migration, law, education, culture and the environment. Hungary was the first Eastern European country to be accepted as a member.

The NAA constitutes the parliament for the Atlantic alliance, in which eastern European states now have associate status. NATO is a collective defence pact between 14 European nations, the USA and Canada; it was founded in 1949 and has an integrated military structure for both conventional and nuclear warfare under a US commander. Although its post-Cold War role has been questioned, Russia, Czechoslovakia, Poland and Hungary have all asked to join NATO, and in 1991 it set up a North Atlantic Cooperation Council to improve dialogue with the newly independent East European states.

The WEU was set up after World War II with the main purpose of integrating a rearmed West Germany into Western defence planning. It consists of nine European members and, though moribund for many years, is now to function as the defence link between NATO and the European Community, a new role which underlines growing European independence from the United States in terms of the military concept of security.

The new situation in Europe has led to recognition of the fact that security does not rest on force alone, or even the threat of force, and that the worst security problem in Europe lies in an economic gap between the two halves of the continent which can lead to threats to attempts to introduce democracy, the risk of ethnic conflict, and migration to the West. The *Economist* has suggested that the first weapon in this battle is advice: on trade, from the European Community; on military reorganization, from NATO through its new Cooperation Council; on the mechanics of constitutional democracy and on the protection of human rights, from the C of E; on civilian control of the defence establishment, from the NAA; and on confidence-building among states, from the CSCE.[22] In view of recent events in the former Yugoslavia, it would seem that confidence-building is perhaps the most urgent of these.

## UN moves towards arms control

During the past 45 years no subject has received more continuous attention at the United Nations than arms limitation and disarmament, and there has been some progress. But world military expenditure is still at an all-time high, armaments have accumulated and become more sophisticated, and some 150 wars, fought with non-nuclear weapons, have taken place since the end of World War II, leaving a death toll of around 20 million persons, most of them civilians. Some 50,000 nuclear weapons remain deployed worldwide, and nuclear proliferation is a continual danger. In recent years reports on the increasing number of countries developing short- and intermediate-range ballistic missiles and seeking to develop or acquire a chemical-weapon capability have given rise to added concern. Conventional arms transfers, too, have been given increased attention since the Gulf War.[23]

Disarmament issues are discussed in the UN General Assembly's First Committee. Subjects on the present agenda include a comprehensive test ban; arms transfers; confidence- and security-building; regional arms and force limitation; measures relating to naval arms and forces; the relationship between environment and security, such as nuclear waste dumping and destruction of chemical weapons; and the impact of scientific and technological advances on armaments and disarmament. The relationship between disarmament and development, use of a 'peace dividend', and problems of conversion from military to civilian production and services, are high on the agenda.

Recently, due to the rapid changes on the international scene, the UN has been called upon to assume new and important responsibilities. For example, for the first time it has been given the responsibility of overseeing the actual destruction of a state's war capabilities (in the case of Iraq) and has established a Special Commission to carry this out. The UN's goal is to enhance security through fewer arms, rather than increasing levels of nuclear and conventional forces, but arms limitation and disarmament cannot be achieved without the political will of Member States and their determined collective effort. 'In this regard', says the world body, 'the UN is but a tool, an instrument which the international community has voluntarily devised to deal with issues that affect humanity. The extent to which this tool is used to good effect lies with the Member States. In the field of disarmament, the potential of this unique and universal organization has yet to be fully realized.'[24]

## International intervention

It has become increasingly clear, as Javier Peréz de Cuéllar, then Secretary-General of the United Nations, said in his Annual Report for 1990, that 'the protection of human rights has now become one of the keystones in the arch of peace. I am ... convinced that it now involves a more concerted exertion of international influence and pressure through timely appeal, admonition, remonstrance or condemnation and, in the last resort, an appropriate United Nations presence, than what was regarded as permissible under traditional international law.'

In a statement to the UN's Commission on Human Rights on 20 February 1992, UN High Commissioner for Refugees Sadako Ogata pointed to human rights violations as a major cause of refugee flows. 'One of my greatest concerns', she said, 'is the growing prevalence of xenophobic and racist actions in many countries. I see this as a profound political and human rights challenge for governments and for the international community as a whole.' Mme Ogata said she was 'firmly convinced that a new multilateral order for cooperation on refugee, migration and humanitarian affairs is emerging, with prevention likely to take on a prime focus in a global, solutions-oriented approach.'

UN and European Community 'interference' in Yugoslavia has shown that uninvited international intervention in the internal affairs of a state, until recently held to be an unacceptable attack on state sovereignty, is now being seen as movement towards the assumption of collective responsibility for peace and human rights as provided for under the Helsinki Final Act of 1975. The promises, and the dangers, of such intervention are seen quite differently by industrialized and developing countries, and are bound to be the subject of heated debate for a long time to come.

Upon his appointment in 1991 as UN Secretary-General, Dr Boutros Boutros-Ghali called for the strengthening of United Nations machinery in a manner that would enable it to ensure the maintenance of international peace and security through peace-keeping, peace-making and peace-building, and to pursue 'an active preventive diplomacy, with a view to monitoring development of crises and devising adequate means to defuse them and prevent their escalation.'

Such preventive diplomacy, for example taking action to ensure that violence in Yugoslavia does not spread to Kosovo and Macedonia, could avoid further tragedy involving other countries such as Albania and Greece. It is widely accepted that the war in the Balkans could have been averted had strong international action been taken in spring 1991, before fighting broke out. Indeed, President Bush was warned in 1990, in a National Intelligence Estimate, that Yugoslavia was likely to break up within eighteen months, but did nothing to warn the Serbs or Croats against violence and 'ethnic cleansing' activities.

The tragedy is that the United Nations, expected to play an ever-growing role in preserving peace in global trouble spots, is facing a deep financial crisis because member states are not paying their share of the operations. As at 31 December 1991, member states owed the United Nations over US$ 800 million, of which US$ 377 million represents overdue peace-keeping assessments; of this amount, the US owed US$ 140 million at the end of 1991, thus remaining the biggest single delinquent.

In June 1992 Dr Boutros-Ghali called for member nations to make available a thousand troops each in order to establish a small, highly mobile standing army able, with Security Council authorization, to respond overnight to civil disorder, enforce cease-fires, cope with natural disasters, facilitate relief and deal impartially with all belligerents. He pointed out that the UN needed better early warning of threats to peace based on timely intelligence from its members, and more formal and informal fact-finding. By agreeing to binding arbitration by the International Court of Justice, he said, most disputes could be resolved without force.

The corollary is the need to establish, and financially provide for, strong cooperative and institutional mechanisms able to deal with emerging problems and so reinforce the conflict-prevention and peace-making capacities of the United Nations.

1    Final paragraph of a Declaration by a panel of eminent persons (including two Nobel Prize laureates), United Nations, New York, April 1986.

2    Final Document, International Conference on the Relationship between Disarmament and Development, New York, 24/8-11/9/87. Doc. A/Conf.130/2, para.14. United Nations, Sales No.E.87.IX.8.

3    John Kenneth Galbraith, 'Weapons and World Welfare', *Development Forum*, Volume XV No.3, April 1987.

4    UN Department for Disarmament Affairs, New York.

5    In a note prepared for the JUNIC/NGO book on *Women and the Environment*, Zed Books, London, 1991.

6    Randy Thomas, 'Ecowar: the untold story of the Gulf Conflict'. *Ecodecision*, March 1992. 276 rue Saint-Jacques Ouest, Bureau 924, Montréal, Quebec, Canada.

7    Official Report, World Women's Congress for a Healthy Planet, Miami, 8-12 November 1991. Women's Environment & Development Organization (WEDO), 845 Third Avenue, New York, NY 10022.

8    A summary of the Report (Fact Sheet No.1), and an information paper in question and answer form, are available from the UN Department for Disarmament Affairs.

9    The International Labour Organization is involved in such studies and has produced a number of publications (see Bibliography). A major study kit, *Making the Connection: Disarmament, Development and Economic Conversion*, is available from the UN Non-Governmental Liaison Service.

10    Based upon an article by Lawrence R. Klein, 'Time again to turn swords into economic gain'. *International Herald Tribune (IHT)*, 9/1/1992.

11    As reported in the *IHT*, 28/2/92.

12    Karl Schoenberger in the *IHT*, 5/1/92.

13    Reported by William J. Broad in the *IHT*, 6/2/92.

14    As reprinted in the *IHT*, 24/2/92.

15    Final Document of the UN Special Session Devoted to Disarmament, 1978, para.5. UN Department for Disarmament Affairs, New York and Geneva.

16    Items 9 and 10 of the Final Document.

17    The full Statement is obtainable from the Women's International League for Peace and Freedom, 1 rue de Varembé, Geneva.

18    Ibid.

19   Final Document, International Conference on the Relationship Between Disarmament and Development, op.cit.

20   Reported in *Compass*, journal of the Society for International Development, February 1990.

21   *IHT*, 24/2/92

22   *The Economist*, 15/2/1992.

23   Disarmament Facts No.78, United Nations, October 1991.

24   Ibid.

# 6. HUMAN RIGHTS AND GLOBAL SECURITY

> ... recognition of the inherent dignity and of the equal and inalienable rights of all members of the human family is the foundation of freedom, justice and peace in the world.
>
> Preamble to the Universal
> Declaration of Human Rights

The concept of human rights as the foundation of peace has long influenced ethical approaches to human relations. Development of the concept during this century has led to acknowledgement in domestic laws and constitutions, and in international instruments, of the right to free speech and thought and to be free from fear and want. But in many instances this is mere lip-service. For example, in spite of the fact that women constitute more than half of the world's population and perform two-thirds of the world's work, the majority continue to be deprived of their basic human rights; it has been estimated that they receive ten per cent of the world's income and own less than one per cent of the world's property.

And yet, already in 1945 in Article I of the UN Charter, it is stated that the purposes of the United Nations are 'to achieve international cooperation in promoting and encouraging respect for human rights and for fundamental freedoms for all without distinction as to race, sex, language or religion.' These purposes were recognized in the Universal Declaration of Human Rights, adopted and proclaimed by the United Nations General Assembly in December 1948,[1] which called for freedom, equity and equality to be the primary guidelines for relations among human beings, whether interpersonal as between women and men, or international as between nations, regions and groupings of nations.

This was closely followed by a Convention for the Suppression of Traffic in Persons and the Exploitation of the Prostitution of Others, adopted in 1949, and in 1951 by a Convention on Equal Remuneration for Men and Women Workers for Work of Equal Value. A Convention on the Political Rights of Women followed in 1952, and another on Discrimination in respect of

Employment and Occupation in 1958. In 1960 an International Convention against Discrimination in Education was adopted, and in 1962 a Convention on Consent to Marriage, Minimum Age of Marriage, and Registration of Marriages. All of these Conventions entered into force within two years of adoption.

The International Covenant on Economic, Social and Cultural Rights was adopted in December 1966, at the same time as an International Covenant on Civil and Political Rights with an Optional Protocol enabling the Human Rights Committee set up in part IV of the Covenant to receive and consider communications from individuals claiming to be victims of violations of any of the rights set forth in the Covenant; both entered into force in early 1976.

These Conventions and Covenants, and the Forward-looking Strategies adopted at the World Conference on Women held in Nairobi in 1985,[2] constitute legal instruments for the realization of the principles contained in the Universal Declaration of Human Rights. These principles also underlie the call for a redressment in the balance of inequality between industrialized and developing nations.

Former US President Jimmy Carter did not mince his words in December 1991 when criticizing US foreign policy as the culprit in many rights abuses. 'The worst human rights abuse in the world is the initiation of war', he said, speaking at the Reebok Human Rights Awards in Boston. 'If you look at the last decade, where have the wars originated? They've originated in the United States. We gave tacit approval to Israel's invasion of Lebanon. We bombed villages around Beirut. We launched a war against Grenada. We invaded Panama. We financed and orchestrated the contra war. We were the leading force in launching a war in Iraq, without any real effort to resolve the issue peaceably.'[3]

Quite apart from the violation of human rights implicit in declarations of war, there is the structural violence which consists of the denial of a human being's right to food, health and economic security, compounded by the fact that poverty is induced and increased by high expenditures, through the arms trade, on the weapons of both state and community violence .

## Arms and the debt problem

Ruth Leger Sivard has pointed out that during the eleven years ending in 1985, when their external debt rose by $580 billion, developing countries imported $250 billion worth of arms, equivalent to over 40 per cent of the additional debt incurred in that period.[4] 'Rising poverty and the lengthening lines of the unemployed contrast with the affluence with which military programs operate.' The problem has been compounded by the cuts imposed on developing countries by the International Monetary Fund (IMF) under structural adjustment programmes, which have fallen more heavily on health, education and food subsidies than on defence.

The impact of these adjustment measures on the social fabric of Third World countries has been dramatic, with the main burden falling on those least able to bear it—the poor and vulnerable, especially women and children. This impact is felt principally among food-deficit farming households, pastoral communities, the landless, the urban unemployed, and those with jobs that do not pay enough for survival. Women are much more vulnerable to poverty than men because of economic and social disadvantages and the burden of unpaid work which falls upon them in most societies. Where women are heads of households, the impact is even more dramatic.

Because of social and gender discrimination, the strategies adopted for structural adjustment have tended not to take into account the vital economic role of women in agriculture, in industry and in the home. Instead of supporting women's productive roles, such strategies have created further obstacles to their economic participation and consequently reinforced the negative effect of such programmes on the most vulnerable. Meanwhile, millions are without jobs in the rich industrialized countries, where relative and absolute poverty have emerged on an unprecedented scale.[5]

## The right to food

Hunger is the violation of a basic human right. It can lead not only to the death of the individual but to social disturbance at local and national levels, and even to international conflict. Due to the debt crisis and a drop in commodity prices, declining *per*

*capita* food production, rising food imports, stagnant agriculture, higher food prices and inadequate distribution of food,
famine and malnutrition are visible trends in several developing
countries, especially where there has been civil war. The main
sufferers, inevitably, have been women and children. Upon
women falls the burden of 'managing' poverty; within the family, men are usually fed first, then the children, and the women
eat what is left—if any.

And yet, women carry the responsibility for feeding their
families. Indeed, authentic global food security depends to a
large extent on women, who are responsible for up to 80 per
cent of all agricultural production in developing countries. Yet
they 'own hardly any land, find it difficult to get loans, and are
overlooked by agricultural advisors and projects,' according to
a UN report.[6]

Food production is only half the problem, nor is it simply a
question of distribution, but of having the income to buy food,
the means to grow it, or the goods to exchange for it. 'Land
reform, employment creation and income levels are therefore as
much a part of improving nutrition as high-yielding varieties of
seeds. No degree of technical advance, for example, can solve
the problem that 80 per cent of Latin America's land is owned
by less than 10 per cent of its people, or that 50 per cent of the
farm land in many parts of Asia is in the hands of less than 10
per cent of the farmers.'[7] Very few of whom, if any, are
women.

The UN's World Food Programme has declared its intention
of making food a more effective aid for women's advancement,
primarily for improved education, employment and health. Food
distribution at health centres brings many poor women together,
giving opportunities for group learning and cooperative action.
Women are eager to earn food as volunteers in community self-
help projects and as part wages in food for work. School
feeding and food assistance to vocational and literacy training
can have enormous benefits for women.

Food aid can be a catalyst to stimulate action by governments
and can be combined with financial and technical aid given by
other organizations. There is, however, an uphill battle to be
fought to change attitudes, at local, national and international
levels, so that women are seen not as passive receivers of food
aid but as active participants in the design and execution of
projects. The issue of food security points to the crucial role of

rural women in providing for that particular basic need, and focuses attention on their suffering in times of armed conflict.

## The health of a nation

Hunger and malnutrition inevitably affect health. Because in many societies female children have lower nutritional status and higher mortality rates than male children, they are more affected by the worsening of health conditions. Women more than men tend to be malnourished and consequently many women in developing nations suffer from nutritional anaemia, a condition which in itself makes child-bearing more taxing and difficult.

Repeated, closely-spaced pregnancies, and pregnancies among very young women barely out of childhood themselves, also impose great stress on the health and well-being of women, especially in the developing nations.[8] When she was Population Minister of Pakistan, Dr Attoya Inayatullah put considerable emphasis on this problem: 'It is intolerable that so many thousands of women are dying painful, lonely deaths in the process of giving life and we are doing so little to stop it. There is no greater indictment of world development efforts than the high rates of maternal death that prevail in much of the world.'[9]

Dr Halfdan Mahler, former Director-General of the World Health Organization, has pointed out that, for the great majority of women of Asia, Africa and Latin America, life consists of ceaseless physical labour and too frequent child-bearing. 'Maternity kills half a million women each year, deaths easily avoidable if health services were adequate', says Dr Mahler. 'A woman in Africa has a life-time risk of dying from pregnancy-related causes 200 times higher than that of women in industrialized countries.'[10]

Recognition of women's right to health is of the utmost importance, not only because it is a basic human right but also because, in a world in which comparatively few people have access to professional medical care, they are the major primary health care providers, not only for their children, but also for the whole family, including the aged and disabled.

## Educating women

Slowing population growth is pinpointed by Ruth Leger Sivard as an effective way to improve people's lives, but family planning receives only a very limited share of government budgets and represents no more than one per cent of official development aid. Educating women, notes Sivard, is a lifeline to better health and enables them to make informed choices in both planning and caring for their families. The relationship between a woman's education and the number of children she bears can be seen vividly in Latin America, where mothers with seven or more years of education average half as many children as uneducated mothers—four less per mother.[11]

And yet, there are countries in which 90 per cent of women over 25 have had no schooling whatsoever; they begin their reproductive years before age 15, have many pregnancies, and bear on average some seven or eight children, many of whom die young. The contrast with industrialized countries is striking; from nearly 100 per cent in most developed countries, the proportion of adult women who are literate drops to a low of three per cent in the least developed.[12]

Statistical studies have shown that there is a literacy gap of 28 per cent, and an educational enrolment gap of 33 per cent, between males and females in the Third World.[13] In other words, a quarter of the female population is illiterate and a third is never enrolled in school. Women—the first educators of the young—cannot help to prepare young minds to be ready to receive and apply the sophisticated knowledge necessary to function constructively in the 20th and 21st centuries if they themselves are ignorant and illiterate. The age of information, as pointed out in a recent newspaper series, and rapid advancements in technology, have already outstripped educational systems geared to an earlier industrial age.[14]

According to Sivard, basic illiteracy is still a serious social problem in the developing world. 'Over half of the adults in the Middle East, South Asia and Africa are illiterate. Despite literacy drives in many countries, the total number of illiterates continues to rise, and faster for women than for men. The lag in women's educational opportunities has wide ramifications for the development process. Not only does it mean the exclusion of a significant portion of the population from its rightful place in society's advance, but in its effect on family, health, population control and the education of children it has a retarding impact on the general pace of development.'[15]

## Breadwinning women

Employment and self-employment, and the income this provides, are essential for the satisfaction of basic needs. High-scale unemployment or the lack of opportunities to earn an adequate income deprive individuals or families of the possibility to obtain food, shelter, education or health care, and consequently represent a violation of human rights. Unemployment also accentuates the gap in living standards between various segments of society, raises frustration levels and may lead to social unrest, civil war or other forms of violence. The right to work is therefore essential for the creation of a just and peaceful society in both economic and social terms; unemployment can itself be seen as an act of violence.

Women's paid work has, for a long time, been considered as supplementary to that of the male head of the family. However, it is now estimated that one-third of the world's families is *de facto* headed by a woman, and that in the poorest segments of the population female earnings are crucial for survival in spite of the presence of a male breadwinner. The access of women to employment or self-employment has therefore become an essential element in combating the growing impoverishment of female-headed or other marginalized households.

The majority of employed women are in low-skill, low-pay, low-status jobs with little job security and many health hazards. They, and those whose labour on family farms, in the informal sector or in the home is unrecognized as 'work' which contributes to national well-being, have extremely limited access to land, credit, technologies, skills and extension services. The resulting income differentials prevent female breadwinners from reaching adequate living standards for themselves and their families. This quasi-institutionalized discrimination, which cuts across all segments of society, contributes to the perpetuation of value systems which tolerate injustice and thereby create a socio-economic environment conducive to violence.

## The plight of the homeless

Housing needs, too, are indicators of a serious structural impediment to economic and social justice which deeply affects women. The plight of the poor urban woman and her family in recent years has demonstrated the disastrous economic and social consequences of the global economic crisis and the inability of nations to meet basic needs while military 'security' continues to consume vast resources.

The homeless are to be seen in most of the major cities of the world. Orphaned and abandoned 'street children' roam the cities of Latin America, Africa and Asia—one of the tragic consequences of excessive military expenditures, urbanization, and structural adjustment measures. It has been said that the number of such street children 'seems to rise as countries become more and more urbanized, and big cities like Calcutta, Nairobi, Marseilles, New York and Bogota are monuments to their plight ... girls may not be as visible in the everyday street life. But they are there. In great numbers. And increasingly so ... If a child is left to the streets and cannot subsist on earnings from working or begging, then he or she must turn to other means for survival.'[16]

The financing of housing, as recognized in paragraph 211 of the Nairobi Forward-looking Strategies, is a major problem for both urban and rural women:

> Housing credit schemes should be reviewed and women's direct access to housing construction and improvement credits secured. In this connection, programmes aimed at increasing the possibilities of sources of income for women should be promoted and existing legislation or administrative practices endangering women's ownership and tenancy rights should be revoked.

## The question of equality

The various measures taken by the United Nations since its foundation in 1945, especially during the International Decade for Women, have contributed significantly to efforts at the national, regional and international levels to achieve the political, economic and social equality of women. In the early 1970s efforts to ensure their equal participation in society were also inspired by 'the awareness that women's reproductive and productive roles were closely linked to the political, economic, social, cultural, legal, educational and religious conditions that constrained the advancement of women, and that factors intensifying the economic exploitation, marginalization and oppression of women stemmed from chronic inequalities, injustices and exploitative conditions at the family, community, national, subregional, regional and international levels.'[17]

The 1985 World Conference held in Nairobi to review and appraise the achievements of the United Nations Decade for Women had three major sub-themes: Equality, Development and Peace. Strategies adopted at that Conference emphasized the linkages between these sub-themes and dealt with constraints on women's rights, including poverty and underdevelopment.[18] They also drew a distinction between *equity* which emphasizes access of all groups to the economic benefits of society, and *equality*, which stresses the social and legal rights of individuals:

> Equality is both a goal and a means whereby individuals are accorded equal treatment under the law and equal opportunities to enjoy their rights and to develop their potential talents and skills, so that they can participate in national political, economic, social and cultural development, and can benefit from its results. For women in particular, equality means the realization of rights that have been denied as a result of cultural, institutional, behavioural and attitudinal discrimination. Equality is important for development and peace because national and global inequities perpetuate themselves and increase tensions of all types.[19]

Thus, while the Strategies emphasize equality between women and men, the concept of equality on which this emphasis is based is that of equality of all individuals, irrespective of the groups to which they belong. The comprehensive notion of 'peace' for which equality is essential also requires the elimination of the full range of social and economic discrimination which impedes human development. Class, tribal and ethnic discrimination, age and/or religious discrimination, racism and *apartheid,* discriminatory international and national economic structures which impedes the development of poor nations—all of these will have to be overcome if we are to achieve a just and viable peace. The question of women's participation in efforts to overcome them will also have to be resolved.

Rural development needs the direct involvement of rural peoples whose lives are to be affected; technical and industrial development must involve technical and industrial workers and potential consumers of the products. Development is a process intended to overcome discrimination, particularly in the economic and social fields, and to provide for the physical, social, intellectual, aesthetic and spiritual development of the human person, and the realization of human dignity. It is inextricably linked to the achievement of a non-violent world, but it will not happen without the equal participation of women, who in many cases—such as electronics production and in agricultural sectors of the developing world—make up a significant portion of the workforce.

Van Ginneken has pointed out that 'the reality for women in many developing countries is that they tend to have low social and economic status and have limited access to education, employment, land credit and technologies. Morever, much of women's work, especially in the agricultural sector with a number of related off-farm activities such as processing and marketing of agricultural and animal produce, is often not considered as economic activity and women carrying out such work are registered as "unpaid family workers" ... Women in many parts of the world have no *de facto* equal access to vocational education and training. Even if equal access exists, young women may still be channelled into training for typical "female" occupations as a consequence of existing value systems. In spite of the changing socio-economic reality, women's training is geared to tasks related to the family, and fails to prepare them for economically viable employment or self-employment.'[20]

There is still a very long way to go before the value of women's contribution to society is fully recognized. One of the most important aspects, the implementation of the legal rights of women throughout the world, is still far from complete. This is so in spite of the fact that a Commission on the Status of Women has been in existence since 1946 with a mandate to study and prepare recommendations on human rights issues of special concern to women, and that a UN Convention on the Elimination of All Forms of Discrimination Against Women was

## HARD-WORKING WOMEN

In some regions such as sub-Saharan Africa, subsistence farming is essentially a female activity, and women are the primary labourers on small farms, where they contribute two-thirds or more of all hours of work. Rural women are also almost exclusively responsible for domestic chores, with the result that their typical day may include 12 -16 hours of work. [They] are employed as wage labourers in agriculture and road construction, or migrate to the cities where they tend to find unskilled and low-paid jobs in the informal sector, in labour-intensive export-oriented industries or as domestic help.

Social and economic planning do not take into account the changing status and position of women, many of whom are now heads of households ... even where women perform the bulk of agricultural work, they seldom have full title to the land and, as a result, they have little access to credit, extension services, technologies and even cooperative organizations.

Job segregation and the corresponding wage differentials between men and women are found in all countries, irrespective of their level of development and socio-economic organization. There are many factors that account for this situation. First, women are often treated unequally when they apply for a job—particularly after a period of absence from the labour force—as well as in their placement, in dismissal and in promotion. Secondly, women are concentrated in sectors and occupations where pay is relatively low. This is the case in industries such as textiles, clothing, leather and food, and in services such as education, health, retail trade and tourism.

Female blue-collar workers are usually found in unskilled and semi-skilled occupations ... while protective legislation sometimes excludes them from certain arduous jobs where wages are relatively high. In addition, managerial positions are still mostly in the hands of men ... Even if women have a full-time job they are still considered mainly responsible for housekeeping and feeding the family, and for bringing up the children and supervising their education. The time and energy spent by women on these domestic tasks can adversely affect their performance on the job, induce absenteeism, discourage them from raising their qualifications and make it difficult for them to pursue a career.

W. Van Ginneken [21]

adopted in 1979—probably the most important of the Conventions concerning the status of women.[22] It entered into force on 3 September 1981.

## Eliminating discrimination

The Preamble to this Convention points out that peace and development require the maximum participation of women on equal terms with men in all fields of life, and it also provides for follow-up, with member states reporting to the UN Committee on the Elimination of Discrimination Against Women (CEDAW) on legislative and other steps taken to implement its provisions. Its first three articles read as follows:

### Article 1

For the purposes of the present Convention, the term 'discrimination against women' shall mean any distinction, exclusion or restriction made on the basis of sex which has the effect or purpose of impairing or nullifying the recognition, enjoyment or exercise by women, irrespective of their marital status, on a basis of equality of men and women, of human rights and fundamental freedoms in the political economic, social, cultural, civil or any other field.

### Article 2

States Parties condemn discrimination against women in all its forms, agree to pursue by all appropriate means and without delay a policy of eliminating discrimination against women and, to this end, undertake:
(a)     to embody the principle of the equality of men and women in their national constitutions or other appropriate legislation if not yet incorporated therein and to ensure, through law and other appropriate means, the practical realization of this principle;
(b)     to adopt appropriate legislative and other measures, including sanctions where appropriate, prohibiting all discrimination against women;
(c)     to establish legal protection of the rights of women on an equal basis with men and to ensure through competent national tribunals and other public institutions the effective protection of women against any act of discrimination;
(d)     to refrain from engaging in any act or practice of discrimination against women and to ensure that public authorities and institutions shall act in conformity with this obligation;
(e)     to take all appropriate measures to eliminate discrimination against women by any person, organization or enterprise;

(f)    to take all appropriate measures, including legislation, to modify or abolish existing laws, regulations, customs and practices which constitute discrimination against women;

(g)    to repeal all national penal provisions which constitute discrimination against women.

## Article 3

States Parties shall take in all fields, in particular in the political, social, economic and cultural fields, all appropriate measures, including legislation, to ensure the full development and advancement of women, for the purpose of guaranteeing them the exercise and enjoyment of human rights and fundamental freedoms on a basis of equality with men.

On the 10th anniversary of its signature, 18 December 1989, the 99 States which had ratified the Convention—among them several permanent members of the Security Council—agreed 'to take all appropriate measures to eliminate discrimination against women in the political and public life of their countries and, in particular, to ensure to women, on equal terms with men, the right: (a) to vote in all elections and public referenda and to be eligible for election to all publicly elected bodies; (b) to participate in the formulation of government policy and the implementation thereof, and to hold public office and perform all public functions at all levels of government; and (c) to participate in non-governmental organizations concerned with the public and political life of the country.'

In his anniversary speech Javier Peréz de Cuéllar, then Secretary-General of the United Nations, called the Convention 'one of the most important legal instruments for the establishment of true gender equality worldwide':

Building on the faith of the Charter in fundamental human rights, in the dignity and worth of the human person, and in the equal rights of men and women, the Convention enjoins States parties to take legal and practical measures to ensure that equal treatment of men and women permeates national law and policy. It sets international standards for the treatment of women in all areas of life and guarantees their right to a life of full equality, to self-development and to full participation in all aspects of society. In spelling out the meaning of equality and how it can be achieved, it not only represents an international bill of rights for women but also provides an agenda for action by countries to guarantee those rights.

Calling upon States that had not yet done so to become parties to the Convention as soon as possible, the Secretary-General encouraged organizations concerned with equality and women's advancement to promote its dissemination, ratification and implementation.

Nevertheless, despite all these efforts at the international level, and the obligations they have laid upon governments, violations of human rights are rampant. According to Jane Frances Connors, 'not only are women denied equality with the balance of the world's population, men, but also they are often denied liberty and dignity and in many situations suffer direct violations of their physical and mental autonomy.'23

The perpetuation of these conditions can in some part be attributed to the fact that 'Women, by virtue of their gender, experience discrimination in terms of denial of equal access to the power structure ... differences such as race, colour and ethnicity may have even more serious implications in some countries, since such factors can be used as justification for compound discrimination.' This paragraph in the Nairobi Strategies points to the condition often referred to as the 'double burden of discrimination' many women carry, being denied the benefits of society on the basis of both sex and race or ethnicity.24

Although world statistics show that more females are born than males, a 1991 census in India showed 92.9 females for every 100 males, and in China 93.8 females for every 100 males. Many of the estimated (worldwide) 100 million 'missing' girls were simply and routinely disposed of at birth, or starved in order to feed their brothers. A recent report by UNICEF has pointed out that more than a million girls die each year simply because they are born female; the cause of death is the disease of discrimination.25

In many parts of the world, the birth of a daughter is greeted with a sigh of disappointment. The German philosopher Karl Marx wrote to his colleague Friedrich Engels in 1851: 'My wife has unfortunately given birth to a daughter, and not a son', and again, in 1855: 'Unfortunately another being of the female sex. Had the child been a boy, I should have rejoiced.26 Birgit Brock-Utne tells of giving birth to a son in Norway in 1962 and

## THE GIRL CHILD

"A boy is for wealth, a girl is for love" is an old [Indian] sub-
continent saying. There is no question that the desire for wealth wins
out. Favouritism towards males begins from birth at the mother's
breast, continues in other areas of nutrition, is exacerbated by unequal
educational paths, and is most noticeable in vastly different work opportunities and workloads as the child matures. Since the girl is
regarded as a "temporary visitor" in the family, destined to become part
of her eventual husband's household, parents spend money on her with
reluctance. A Telugu saying neatly sums up this attitude, describing
"bringing up a girl as being the same as watering a plant in your
neighbour's garden" ... During adolescence and early adulthood, women
have a triple burden—reproduction, domestic work and harsher
productive work than men—all contributing to their lower survival
rates. In addition [they] suffer from inferior nutrition since females
usually eat last and least.

Lynn Bennett, a World Bank specialist in women's development,
notes that the major social distinctions between the roles of boys and
girls is imbedded at puberty ... the coming of manhood signals an
opening up of the boy's world [but] a girl is confined and segregated
from the outside world for 12 days at the onset of menstruation ...

If the girl does reach maturity, she is prone to death in childbirth
because of stunted development, or early and too frequent pregnancies.
And at times she is the victim of physical abuse from her husband or
even his family, especially if they are unhappy with the dowry
payment provided by her parents ... In extreme but rare cases,
unhappiness over the dowry can lead to killing of the wife, a practice
known as bride-burning,[27] a modern twist on the ancient practice of
'sati' or widow-burning, which was common until the turn of the century. Under this practice, widows voluntarily mounted their husband's
funeral pyre and allowed themselves to be burned to death on the basis
that they no longer had an identity because of the death of their mate—
a telling comment on the value of a woman's life in the society.

So, from birth to death, the sub-continent woman has lived in a
man's world, even more than her sisters elsewhere in the world. Under
such conditions girls develop a poor self-image, and when they become mothers they perpetuate the same cycle with their daughters.

Adapted from *Intercom* No.55, January 1990[28]

being told by the girl in the next hospital bed that her husband had indicated that he would only come to visit her if she gave birth to a son; the farm where she lived would hoist a flag if a boy was born, but not for a girl.[29]

More than legislation is needed if discrimination against women is to be eliminated. It requires constant struggle and advocacy by concerned individuals and organizations, active co-operation by national and local authorities, the involvement of legal and judicial bodies, and ongoing monitoring by the community. Because such discrimination and abuse is often based upon cultural patterns and economic deprivation, correcting it is a matter of social justice and requires a concerted effort to improve information and education with regard to internationally recognized human rights and their applicability to that half of the human race constituted by women.

---

1    Under GA resolution 217 A (III) of 10/12/48.

2    World Conference to Review and Appraise the Achievements of the United Nations Decade for Women: Equality, Development and Peace. Nairobi, 15-26/7/85. UN Sales No. E.85.IV.10.

3    As reported in the *International Herald Tribune (IHT)*, 12/12/91.

4    Ruth Leger Sivard, *World Military and Social Expenditures*, World Priorities, Box 25140, Washington DC 20007, 1986.

5    See: *Women and the World Economic Crisis*, Zed Books, London, 1991.

6    *State of the World's Women* Report 1985.

7    Quoted in *Women and the World Economic Crisis*, op.cit.

8    Ruth Leger Sivard,*Women ... a World Survey*. World Priorities, Box 25140, Washington DC 20007, 1983.

9    As quoted in UNICEF's *State of the World's Children 1989*.

10    Ibid.

11    Sivard, Ruth Leger, *World Military and Social Expenditures*. World Priorities Inc., Box 25140, Washington DC 20007, 1991.

12    Sivard, Ruth Leger, *Women ... a World Survey*, op.cit.

13    *INSTRAW NEWS*, No.7, UN Institute for Training and Research on the Advancement of Women, Dominican Republic.

14    *Christian Science Monitor*, Boston, 22,23,24/7/87.

15    Ruth Leger Sivard, *World Military and Social Expenditures 1986*, op.cit.

16    Jesper Morch, 'Abandoned and Street Children,' *Ideas Forum* No.18, UNICEF 1984.

17   Nairobi Forward-looking Strategies, paragraph 1.

18   Ibid. paragraph 44.

19   Ibid. paragraph 11.

20   Extracts from 'Promotion of Equality', W. van Ginneken. *Women at Work* I/86, International Labour Organization, Geneva-

21   Ibid.

22   Adopted and opened for signature, ratification and access by General Assembly resolution 34/180, 18/12/79.

23   Jane Frances Connors, *Violence Against Women in the Family*. UN/CSDHA, Vienna, 1989. UN Sales No.E.89.IV.5.

24   Nairobi Forward-looking Strategies, paragraph 46.

25   *The State of the World's Children 1992*. UNICEF, New York.

26   Quoted in Birgit Brock-Utne, *Educating for Peace*. Pergamon Press, 1985.

27   According to *The European*, 12 March 1992, 15,891 brides were killed or committed suicide in 1988-91 because their in-laws accused them of not bringing in enough cash, jewellery and goods, although dowry demands were outlawed in 1961.

28   A UNICEF New Delhi publication.

29   Ibid.

# 7. ACHIEVING VISIBILITY

> There can be no acting or doing of any
> kind, till it be recognized that there is a
> thing to be done; the thing once recog-
> nized, doing in a thousand shapes becomes
> possible.
>
> Thomas Carlyle[1]

The selection of peace as one of the three main themes of the
United Nations Decade for Women 1975-85 (the others being
equality and development), and the emphasis given to this theme
in the Forward-looking Strategies for the Advancement of
Women adopted by the World Conference in Nairobi in 1985,
are indications of women's concern with regard to the human
suffering and waste of resources in warfare and the continued
tendency to try to resolve conflicts by aggressive means.[2] That
concern, however, remains muted for as long as women are not
counted among the decision-makers.

Women are far too 'invisible' in official decision-making
processes on peace and disarmament, or in decisions concerning
allocation of resources for this purpose. It is mainly through
non-governmental activities that they have been able to be effective in bringing to public attention the disarmament opportunities
contained in proposals for alternative security systems, for
example the concept of a standing UN Peacekeeping Force and
the strengthening of United Nations capacities in relation to
disarmament, a subject which is now engaging the full attention
of the international community in its search for authentic global
security.

But women's voices are also too seldom heard with regard to
the growing aggressiveness of society at the local, family and
individual levels, including the treatment accorded to immigrants, attacks on 'guest-workers', etc. The interrelatedness of
all forms of violence, from individual to global, must be recognized and the problem attacked at all levels if progress is to be
made in achieving a 'kinder, gentler society'.[3]

## The roots of violence

Both men and women suffer in a world permeated by violence. Both are victimized by structural violence when racism, *apartheid*, sexism, torture, foreign domination, tribal and ethnic oppression, poverty or other types of discrimination and deprivation impede their people's development. They are both, particularly in childhood and old age, at the mercy of warfare's lack of discrimination between combatants and civilians. Children of both sexes have been victims of child abuse.

And yet, in the main, their experiences of violence differ. Men are involved more with the direct violence of armed combat and aggressive and criminal acts, and with interpersonal violence.[4] Although women may also experience such violence they are more often victimized by forms of aggression peculiar to women's experience. For example, they may be subjected to domestic violence, battery, sexual and emotional abuse, rape and incest. They may be discriminated against by employers and suffer sexual harassment in the workplace; despite long, gruelling hours in factories and on farms, conditions which exploit their desperation may make it impossible for female heads of families to meet their own and their children's basic needs.

Ending discrimination against women and achieving peace are interdependent, virtually inseparable goals. Justice for all and effective development require women's full participation. Women's circumstances so profoundly affect the welfare of world society that they can be seen, in themselves, to illustrate the vital importance, to all of humanity, of the relationship between peace and economic and social justice.

Some scholars assert that it is in the separation of human values into categories of masculine and feminine, as a way of making social and cultural distinctions between men and women, that the roots and the perpetuation of violence are to be found.[5] Disregard of women's perspectives is seen as a cause for the emphasis on war and conflict in recorded history. Unless there is radical change, the young girls of today will continue to be the majority of tomorrow's poor and the minority in policy-making councils which have the power to commit the world's wealth and technology either to warfare or to the achievement of a just, non-violent world.

But what are women's perspectives? The question has aroused hot debate between feminists and academics exploring the differences between the sexes. Harvard psychoanalyst Carol Gilligan suggests that the sexes have different moral voices. Men tend to adhere to abstract principles such as justice and logic, she argues, while women focus more on human relationships, reconciliation of opposing views and consideration of how decisions will affect others; biology and the social role of motherhood may make women different, but not inferior.[6]

## Sexual stereotypes

Sex role separation has imposed value distinctions between men and women under which women accept their subordination and men assume power and the right to pursue their goals aggressively. Many societies encourage women to be dependent and submissive, and men to be dominant and aggressive. Such behaviour is constantly reinforced by society when violence erupts and the passive are victimized.

While this kind of behaviour may be controlled by social norms and laws, the values and attitudes which produce and in turn feed upon them are not so easily controlled. Indeed, they are often openly and fully manifest, as can be seen in the media. In films, textbooks, newspapers and on television, women are frequently portrayed in traditional roles as mothers and housewives, in subordinate roles such as domestic workers, in frivolous roles such as fashion plates and sex objects, or negatively as temptresses and shrews.[7]

Even in the case of women heads of state, the media frequently find it necessary to comment on their clothing, appearance or family status. The same media glorify war, portray violence as necessary, combat as exhilarating and aggression as natural—particularly to men—and reinforce the stereotypes which continue to cast women in the roles of dependents and victims, but do not show them as full participants in public affairs. Such glorification of violence and denigration of women serves to perpetuate the acceptance both of warfare and of women's status as second-class citizens.[8]

Sexual stereotypes are often reinforced by the toys parents buy for their toddlers: cars, airplanes and toy soldiers for boys, dolls, prams, and stuffed animals for girls. Such playthings, chosen for young children before they can choose their own, convey a message which tends to condition the recipient.

## Images in advertising

In a paper prepared for a UN Workshop of Experts on Prevention and Rehabilitation Schemes for Young Women in Prostitution and Related Occupations in Bangkok, June 1985, Truong Than-Dam of the Institute of Social Studies in The Hague pointed out that prevailing forms of tourism tend increasingly to incorporate prostitutes' services in various forms as a component of the tourist product. She emphasized that the commercialization of female sexuality is an expression of the relationships of inequality between sex and class, and that long-term policies must focus on rectifying this inequality. Among her recommendations was that laws on the use of women's image in advertising, which often promotes Asian women as available and exotic temptresses, be reviewed: 'Images in advertising are not simply beautiful photographs. They constitute particular ideological products made by the media to condition human behaviour. The advertising industry is very significant, not only in terms of its size but also because it has become an indispensable adjunct of global corporate capital in all economic sectors.'[9]

Women, because of cultural factors, are more vulnerable to lower-paying or dehumanizing or debilitating working conditions, which can encourage prostitution. As pointed out by a Special Rapporteur appointed by the United Nations, involuntary prostitution inevitably is a form of structural violence since it involves use of power and coercion over women. The selling of young girls into domestic service can lead to the sexual exploitation of the children in the employer's family and later to their drifting into prostitution.[10] Truong Than-Dam suggests using different forms of media to conscientize the public about its responsibility, direct or indirect, in sustaining the institution of prostitution.

## Women's participation in decision-making

As we have seen, the Charter of the United Nations presupposed that war could be avoided only if the dignity and worth of the human person—including equal rights of men and women—could be affirmed, international law maintained, and social progress and better living standards promoted.

Since the Charter came into being on 24 October 1945 new grassroots organizations and less formal movements have sprung up all over the world, involving millions more in global efforts for peace and justice. Women hugging trees to prevent the deforestation of Asia, mothers demonstrating against torture and disappearance in Latin America, nuns kneeling before tanks to prevent violence against people struggling for their liberation from dictatorships, women enduring their own and their husbands' imprisonment for actions against *apartheid*, women of all ages marching against nuclear weapons—all are evidence of a new, purposeful and vigorous women's movement for justice and peace.

Hilkka Pietilä's paper 'Women's Peace Movement as an Innovative Proponent of the Peace Movement as a Whole' provides significant insights into women's perspectives on the issues of war and violence and the need for these perspectives in reaching a deeper, more adequate analysis of the problem.[11] As she points out, the coming together of women within official government structures, formal non-governmental organizations, people's movements and grassroots activists constitutes a new and impressive force.

The UN Declaration on the Participation of Women in Promoting International Peace and Cooperation, proclaimed on 3 December 1982, is a standard-setting instrument with moral force but is not legally binding on member states. Nevertheless, its Article 12 identified the following crucial steps to be taken at national and international levels:

- Qualitative and quantitative increase in women's participation in the sphere of international relations.
- Rendering solidarity and support to women victims of violations of human rights, e.g. *apartheid*, racial discrimination, colonialism, foreign occupation.
- Encouragement of women's participation in NGO and intergovernmental organizations aimed at the strengthening of international peace and security.
- Provision of practical opportunities for the effective participation of women in promoting international peace and cooperation, economic development and social progress

including, to that end: equitable representation of women in governmental and non-governmental functions including the Secretariats of the United Nations system, in diplomatic service, on delegations to national regional or international meetings, and at all levels within the secretariats of the United Nations and the specialized agencies in conformity with Article 101 of the Charter of the United Nations.[12]

In 1985 the Nairobi Forward-looking Strategies again stressed the question of women's participation in the decision-making process, paragraph 240 making it clear that women and men have an equal right and the same vital interest in contributing to international peace and cooperation:

Women should participate fully in all efforts to strengthen and maintain international peace and security and to promote international cooperation, diplomacy, the process of détente, disarmament in the nuclear field in particular, and respect for the principles of the Charter of the United Nations, including respect for the sovereign rights of States, guarantees of fundamental freedoms and human rights such as recognition of the dignity of the individual and self-determination, and freedom of thought, conscience, expression, association, assembly, communication and movement without distinction as to race, sex, political and religious beliefs, language or ethnic origin. The commitment to remove the obstacles to women's participation in the promotion of peace should be strengthened.[13]

The Strategies emphasize that the need for women's perspective on human development is critical to human enrichment and progress; paragraph 13 insists that peace 'embraces the whole range of actions reflected in concerns for security and implicit assumptions of trust between nations, social groups and individuals':

Peace cannot be realized under conditions of economic and sexual inequality ... deliberate exploitation of large sectors of the population, unequal development of countries and exploitative economic relations ... Peace is promoted by the equality of sexes, economic equality and the universal enjoyment of basic human rights and fundamental freedoms. Its enjoyment by all requires that women be enabled to exercise their right to participate on an equal footing with men in all spheres of the political, economic and social life of their respective countries, particularly in the decision-making process, while exercising their right to freedom of opinion, expression, information and association in the promotion of international peace and cooperation.

Paragraph 235 of the Strategies insists that: 'Universal and durable peace cannot be attained without the full and equal participation of women in international relations, particularly in decision-making concerning peace, including the processes envisaged for the peaceful settlement of disputes under the Charter of the United Nations', and paragraph 237 considers it 'evident that women all over the world have manifested their love for peace and their wish to play a greater role in international cooperation, amity and peace among different nations. All obstacles at national and international levels in the way of women's participation in promoting international peace and cooperation should be removed as soon as possible.'

**The invisibility problem**

The fact that the Strategies were adopted unanimously at the UN Decade's World Conference in Nairobi makes implementation at the national level obligatory on the part of all the governments which participated in the Conference. Unfortunately, it would seem that there has been little significant change with regard to women's involvement in the formal governmental and intergovernmental process since a publication prepared by UNESCO for the Mid-Decade Conference in Copenhagen in 1980, which stated that: 'In spite of much discussion and exhortation, women continue to be chronically under-represented in international decision-making.'[14]

Women's absence in these processes is directly related to their absence from the highest levels of national decision-making, the level at which the most significant decisions on issues of peace and security are currently taken. During the entire UN Decade for Women there was, according to a 1985 report by the Inter-Parliamentary Union (IPU), less than a two per cent increase in women representatives in parliamentary assemblies.[15] Since 1985, both the number and the percentage of women parliamentarians has actually declined. A study undertaken by the IPU into 96 national parliaments showed that only 11 per cent of parliamentarians in the world in 1991 were women.[16]

Few nations have had women national leaders, and even those who have attained the highest office have made little visible effort to appoint more women to cabinet-level or other positions related to security policy. Gerald Mische has attributed this to the structural and systems constraints on all heads of state, including women leaders.[17] And yet the few women who have served in these security positions, such as Inga Thorssen of Sweden, have made outstanding contributions, especially in the field of disarmament.

So, too, women have seldom served as heads of government delegations or sat on the Security Council or have been equally represented in committees dealing with disarmament, security and conflict resolution. Only one woman has ever sat as a judge on the International Court of Justice[18] and no woman has ever been a member of the International Law Commission. They are still vastly under-represented on all UN human rights bodies except CEDAW, the committee which monitors the implementation of the Convention on the Elimination of All Forms of Discrimination against Women, and that is because it has an all-women membership. In 1991 there were two women out of 18 on the Economic, Social and Cultural Rights Commitee, one out of 18 on the Committee on the Elimination of Racial Discrimination, two out of 18 on the Human Rights Committee, and two out of 10 on the Committee against Torture. Of the 26 members of the Sub-Commission on Prevention of Discrimination and Protection of Minorities only six are women.[19]

Even within the staff of the United Nations system women are still sorely under-represented at the professional level and are raising their voices to draw attention to the fact that the United Nations bureaucracy is not implementing its own Charter, which states that there should be 'no restrictions on the eligibility of men and women to participate in any capacity and under conditions of equality in its principal and subsidiary organs.'[20]

Their efforts have met with some success; in May 1990 the UN's Economic and Social Council adopted, without a vote, resolutions requesting the Secretary-General to take the necessary steps to ensure that 35 per cent of United Nations professional posts would be held by women by 1995, and recommending that governments introduce measures to make women full partners in national decision-making through such activities as campaigns to inform women of their political rights. It has now been decided that a world conference will be held in 1995, 10 years after the end of the UN Decade for Women, to review progress in implementing these resolutions and the Nairobi Strategies.

## The UN Commission on the Status of Women

The intergovernmental body responsible for the implementation of the Nairobi Forward-looking Strategies is the UN Commission on the Status of Women, whose 32 member states meet annually to debate the priority themes for each of the goals of the Strategies.  It also has a mandate to include regular monitoring and review and appraisal of their implementation, and has devised a system to carry this out at international and national levels. For the period 1988-92 its themes have included:

- Access to information, education for peace, and efforts to eradicate violence against women within the family and society.
- Full participation of women in the construction of their countries and in the creation of just social and political systems.
- Women in areas affected by armed conflicts, foreign intervention, alien/colonial domination, foreign occupation and threats to peace.
- Refugee and displaced women and children.
- Equal participation in all efforts to promote international cooperation, peace and disarmament.

The Commission provides policy guidance to Member States and to the UN system in order to ensure full implementation of the Nairobi Strategies by the year 2000. To support this work, and in preparation for the 1995 World Conference on Women, a peace policy analysis is being prepared, the main lines of which concern:

**(a) Participation of women in decision-making processes related to peace and disarmament at national, regional and world levels:**   the primary objective here is to present the situation of women in concrete, measurable terms on the basis of reliable data specifically collected for this purpose, to conduct thorough analyses leading to identification of obstacles, and to make recommendations for overcoming them. A case study on decision-making related to peace and disarmament in Sweden has already been initiated in regard to national decision-making processes. At the regional level two case studies, namely 'Participation of Women in the Talks on Mutual Reduction of Armed Forces and Armaments and Associated Measures in Central Europe', and the 'Vienna Meeting in 1986 of Representatives of the Participating States of the Conference on Security and Cooperation', are now in progress.

**(b) Education for peace:** this is another key area. The study interprets education for peace as a lifelong process which should take place worldwide in every situation, in every structure and process through which people and societies learn and conduct their private and public affairs, and it is based on the assumption that women should participate fully in this process. They should do so both as contributors and beneficiaries, with *inter alia* equal access to information, education and political participation. Such participation would also enrich educational, political and social processes and, consequently, society generally with the female values, attitudes and experience without which they remain incomplete.

Jane Frances Conners has said that 'long-term change in the social structure will only occur as a result of education. Education is the carrier of traditional norms and values and has played a crucial role in the crystallization of the female and male stereotype ... It can, however, act as a positive force for change and progress. Education in schools from the primary stage must be geared to eliminate stereotypical social, economic and cultural roles of women and men. The subject of family violence should be part of family life education and methods of peaceful conflict resolution advocated.'[21] Steps in this direction have already been taken in Australia and Canada, where kits have been developed for school teachers for teaching about non-violent relationships.

(c) **Violence within the family and society:** this part of the peace policy analysis concerns the effect of conflict in society on women, particularly as expressed in various forms of violence against women. The inter-connections between violence in the family, in society, and at the international level are only beginning to be explored. An expert group meeting held on the subject in December 1986 explored many dimensions of the problem of violence in the family, and this led to the publication, in 1989, of *Violence Against Women in the Family*, by the UN Division for the Advancement of Women in Vienna.[22] This office, part of the UN Centre for Social Development and Humanitarian Affairs, prepares in-depth reports for review by the Commission on the Status of Women, and also serves as the secretariat of CEDAW.

A world at peace would reflect a social environment conducive to the full development of the human person and of a society sufficiently mature to resolve conflict without violence. Such a social environment must begin in the home. It is obvious that children raised in an atmosphere of domestic violence will assume that force is the natural means of settling disputes. The giving of war toys to children is another potent force for raising aggressive offspring, as is violence in the media. Violent films and television programmes are believed to have contributed to the extraordinary increase in societal and personal aggression in recent years (see Chapter 9).

Most would agree that peace will be lasting only to the degree that it is a just peace, fair to all the Earth's peoples, and viable, acceptable to all nations and peoples. Vigorous efforts by the United Nations, non-governmental organizations, people's movements and individual citizens are now underway to define and achieve specific economic and social changes which will make the world more just and increase the areas of agreement between nations and peoples. The following chapter shows what women in peace movements, in social work, in research, in provincial and national politics and in international organizations, have done and are still doing to bring about a non-violent world.[23]

1    Thomas Carlyle, *Chartism*, 1839.

2    World Conference of the UN Decade for Women (Equality, Development, Peace). Forward-looking Strategies for the Advancement of Women, Nairobi 1985.

3    A pre-election campaign promise by President George Bush of the United States.

4    These points have been made, among others, by Jean B. Elshtain in *Women and War*, Riane Eisler in *The Chalice and the Blade*, and Betty Reardon in *Sexism and the War System* (see Bibliography).

5    Ibid.

6    Quoted by Nina Easton in 'Can the Women's Movement March into the Mainstream?' *Los Angeles Times Magazine*, 2/2/92.

7    Betty Reardon in the UN/NGO kit on 'Women and Peace'.

8    Ibid.

9    Truong Than-Dam, *Virtue, Order, Health and Money : Towards a comprehensive perspective on female prostitution in Asia.* United Nations ST/ESCAP/388. See also Thurot and Thurot, 1983; and Consumers' Association of Penang, 1983.

10    Report of Jean Fernand-Laurent, Special Rapporteur on the suppression of the traffic in persons and the exploitation of the prostitution of others. United Nations, 1985.

11    Paper prepared for the Second International Interdisciplinary Congress on Women, Groningen, Netherlands, 17-21/4/84.

12    Resolution 37/63, adopted 3/12/82.

13    Forward-looking Strategies for the Advancement of Women, para. 240.

14    Scilla McLean, 'The role of women in the promotion of friendly relations between nations', *The Role of Women in Peace Movements.* Unesco, Paris, 1980.

15    *Distribution of seats by sex in parliamentary assemblies: a bilingual survey of 142 countries with a parliament as at 30 June 1985.* Inter-Parliamentary Union, Geneva.

16    *Distribution of Seats Between Men and Women in National Parliaments.* Inter-Parliamentary Union, Geneva, 1991.

17    Gerald Mische, 'The Feminine and World Order', *Breakthrough*, Fall 1986, pp. 43-4.

18    Mme Suzanne Bastid was a judge *ad hoc* in the Case Concerning the Continental Shelf (Tunisia v. Libya), 1985 ICJ REP.192.

19    See: Charlesworth, Chinkin and Wright, 'Feminist Approaches to International Law', *American Journal of International Law*, Vol.85.

20    The Charter of the United Nations, Article 8.

21   Jane Frances Connors, 'Violence in the Family', 1989, study prepared for the United Nations in Vienna.

22   UN Centre for Social Development and Humanitarian Affairs, Vienna. UN Sales No.E.89.IV.5.

23   For further information on what the UN has done for women, see Hilkka Pietilä and Jeanne Vickers, *Making Women Matter*. Zed Books, London, 1990.

# 8.  WOMEN IN ACTION

> There is in every true woman's heart a
> spark of heavenly fire, which lies dormant
> in the broad daylight of prosperity, but
> which kindles up and beams and blazes in
> the dark hour of adversity.
>
> Washington Irving[1]

Aristophanes' *Lysistrata* demonstrates that even in ancient
Greece there was a linkage between women and peace;  the sex
strike they declared until such time as the men had stopped
fighting precipitated the end of the war. Women in more recent
times have adopted similar tactics; in 1986 Finnish women led
by Marjo Linkkonen petitioned the Ministry of Trade and
Commerce, declaring that they would bear no children until
Finland changed its pro-nuclear energy policy.[2]

Elise Boulding has said that there has always been a
*Lysistrata* component in the fight for peace by women's
organizations,[3] while Birgit Brock-Utne has listed three main
characteristics of that fight:  it is connected to the concern for
human life, especially for children, but also for themselves and
other women;  it makes use of a varied set of non-violent
techniques, acts, strategies; and it is transpolitical, often transnational, aimed at reaching other women in the opposite camp.[4]

The first women's peace societies were established in
England in 1820 and in America during the 1830s. In 1848 the
first international peace congress was held in Brussels, a
congress which not only recognized women as participants but
even allowed them to speak!  By the mid-19th century the first
women's international publication, *Sisterly Voices*, was being
issued by the Anglo-American women's peace societies. In
1900 an International Peace Bureau was established in Berne,
and by 1915 an International Women's Peace Movement had
taken shape.  By that time women had gained the right to vote in
national elections on the same basis as men in many countries,
with New Zealand and Australia leading the way in 1893 and
1902 respectively.[5]

In the 19th century women advocated the settling of disputes
through law and arbitration, and in the present century they have
taken even stronger and more deliberate action. In many

instances they have been instrumental in preventing and ending hostilities, as informal negotiators, campaigners and demonstrators.

## Peace Prizewinners

One major activist, Austrian author Bertha von Suttner, devoted her life to the fight for peace. Born in Prague in 1843 into an aristocratic family which later fell on hard times, she became a governess to four girls whose brother she later married, after a brief period as private secretary to Alfred Nobel. Bertha later became a well-known author, achieving fame with her anti-war novel *Die Waffen nieder* (*Lay Down Your Arms*), written in 1889 in order to help a new peace movement which had just been created in London, the International Peace and Arbitration Association. Besides writing, speaking and arranging peace congresses, she travelled from one country to another to persuade influential people to support the fight for peace, and remained in touch with Alfred Nobel, whom she inspired to establish his Peace Prize. In 1905 she became its first recipient.[6]

Other women awarded the Nobel Peace Prize have included Jane Addams, a US social worker;  Emily Greene Balch, Professor at Wellesley College in the USA; Marie Sklodowska Curie, the Polish-born French scientist, who received it twice; Mairead Corrigan and Betty Williams of Ireland; Alva Myrdal, the Swedish economist; Mother Theresa, the Yugoslav-born nun; Lady Rama Rao of India;  and, in 1991, Aung San Suu Kyi, who is still under house arrest in Myanmar (Burma).

Some of these women, with others such as Aleta Jacobs, the first woman doctor in Holland; Anita Augsberg and Lida Gustava Heymann, prominent peace activists in Germany; Rosika Schwimmer, a well-known Hungarian writer, and Jeannette Rankin, the first woman elected to the US Congress and the only member of that Congress to vote against US participation, tried to stave off World War I.  The International Women's Suffrage Alliance presented a peace petition to the UK government in July 1914 on behalf of 12 million women in 26 countries, and in April 1915 1,000 women attended an International Congress of Women held at The Hague.

That Congress resulted in the foundation of the Women's International League for Peace and Freedom, whose first Presi-

dent was Jane Addams and first Secretary-General was Emily
Greene Balch. Although their efforts cost Rankin her seat in the
US Congress and Balch her post at Wellesley College, WILPF
is still active on all continents and is the only truly international
women's organization solely devoted to work for peace.

The War Resisters League was founded in 1923 by three
women: Jesse Wallace Hughan, Tracy Mygatt and Frances
Witherspoon. Other famous peace activists include Clara Zetkin,
a great women's leader in Germany and of international socialist
women's activities. She was editor of the journal *Gleichheit
(Equality)*, which had more than 100,000 subscriptions, and
was one of the initiators of International Women's Day
(8 March) which now unites women in a joint action day for
peace and women's rights in all continents of the world.
Another was Rosa Luxemburg, a passionate orator and fighter
against militarism, colonialism and war.

Many Russian women, such as Nadezhda Krupskaya, have
been active in the struggle for peace and women's rights, following the example set by Alexandra Kollontay, who undertook
speaking tours against World War I in many Western European
countries. Since the early 1960s Soviet women have convened
conferences and discussed ways in which they could work
together. Soviet cosmonaut Valentina Tereshkova, the first
woman in space, has been a vigorously articulate spokesperson
for peace and disarmament.[7]

## Campaigning for peace

These women come from a long line of women advocates of
disarmament. Indeed, in spite of being so under-represented in
disarmament negotiations, women have been extremely active in
the use of petitions and other tools to influence the disarmament
process. Already in 1932, in preparation for the World
Disarmament Conference held that year, women collected nine
million signatures on a petition urging steps to achieve total and
universal disarmament.

Women have been in the forefront of the anti-nuclear movement since the dropping of bombs on Hiroshima and Nagasaki.
In 1959 a conference on the responsibility of women in the
atomic age was held in Brunate, Italy, by the newly formed
European Movement of Women against Nuclear Armament,

which grouped women of all political persuasions from both east and west. Women played a significant role in arousing and organizing the public in massive educational and petition campaigns in support of a treaty to ban nuclear testing, which resulted in the Partial Test Ban Treaty of 1963.

In 1964 a new peace movement was started in the United States, calling itself Women Strike for Peace, and in the same year women from many countries demonstrated at a NATO conference in Scheveningen, in the Netherlands, against plans to set up a multilateral nuclear force. In April 1978, in preparation for the First Special Session of the UN General Assembly Devoted to Disarmament, some 80 women from different countries met in Vienna to discuss action and to formulate a message to the United Nations.

The late Josephine Pomerance, in whose honour the NGO Disarmament Committee at United Nations headquarters in New York presents an annual award for contributions to disarmament within the UN system, was a major organizer of such efforts. The idea for a nuclear freeze is credited to a woman, Randall Forsberg, and it was women who made it a major international campaign.

Nordic Women for Peace brought half a million signatures, and German women a further 100,000, to the International Women's Decade Conference in Copenhagen in 1980. One outstanding Scandinavian, Inga Thorsson, former Swedish Minister of State for Disarmament, has devoted 50 years of her life to the peace movement and was president of the UN's First Review Conference of the Nuclear Proliferation Treaty in 1975. Her 1982 Report to the Second Special Session of the UN General Assembly devoted to Disarmament in 1982 on the Economic and Social Consequences of Disarmament made it clear that while women, the poor and the vulnerable suffer most, the quality of life for all is reduced by arms spending. Women inspired and organized public support for this Special Session, in one of the greatest peace demonstrations in history.

In 1984 the Women's International League for Peace and Freedom launched a worldwide signature campaign for a comprehensive test ban treaty as an important step to halt the arms race. Many organizations, including politically active pressure groups such as the Women for Mutual Security, Churchwomen United, and the Women's World Summit Foundation—established to provide a women's alternative to the Summit meetings of world leaders—have actively supported such campaigns.

Meetings have been arranged by women in all walks of life in order to deepen their knowledge and offer each other support in realizing their hopes and visions. A number of these have been international, such as the Conference of Women in Europe in Action for Peace, held in Amsterdam in November 1981, in which more than 500 women took part, and those held in Halifax, Nova Scotia, in June 1985 and in Wisconsin in 1987. In April 1986, taking advantage of the convening by the UN Secretary-General of a panel of eminent personalities to explore disarmament and development issues, women's non-governmental committees at United Nations headquarters in New York organized a public forum in order to involve a broader group of people in discussion of the issues.

At the United Nations Office in Geneva, too, women's groups are an energizing force of the NGO community and take a leading and active part in disarmament affairs. Every year on 8 March, when millions of women around the world celebrate International Women's Day, they bring together grassroots peace activists to discuss UN efforts towards peace and disarmament and to meet with disarmament negotiators and members of the UN Conference on Disarmament. In 1985 the International Women's Peace Camp in Geneva was reactivated, to remind such delegates that women have concerns for disarmament which run deep and strong and that women are still underrepresented in arms negotiations.

Although women have been so active in peace campaigns only three so far have been winners of the annual UNESCO Prize for Peace Education: Helena Kekkonen, a Finnish educator, in 1981, Laurence Deonna, a Swiss journalist/author, in 1987, and Mother Theresa of Calcutta, in 1992.

## Action at the grassroots

Women have been the main activists in 'grassroots consciousness-raising' about the arms race. Third World women's networks, such as DAWN (Development Alternatives with Women for a New Era), AAWORD (Association of African Women for Research and Development), and WAND (Women and Development) in the Caribbean and Latin America, which have created powerful coalitions of women concerned with development issues, have undertaken invaluable research with regard to women's participation and the relationship between development and disarmament.

For more than 30 years women in all continents have demonstrated against nuclear policies and the use of force, and some of the most effective actions have been at the local level. Women have marched from Copenhagen to Paris, from Stockholm to Minsk and on to Vienna, from Oslo to Washington, through Latin America, Africa and Asia, calling for a halt to arms production and for disarmament and peace. Many, like the activitists of Greenham Common, have spent years in encampments to protest nuclear arms, making their special witness for peace.

Helen Caldicott of Australia (and the United States) has led American doctors and physicians in raising public awareness of the dangers of nuclearization. Karen Silkwood died for her efforts to expose faulty welding in the fuel rods produced by the company she was working for—the largest uranium producer in the United States.

In November 1983 thousands of American women demonstrated in front of the Pentagon, calling for 'No more war'; 43 of them were sentenced to 10 days in prison or held for trial. And in the same month Australian Women for Survival organized a peace camp outside Pine Gap, the US satellite communications base, to express their solidarity with the peace movement in the US and Europe in the struggle against deployment of Pershing II missiles in West Germany and Cruise missiles in Britain and in Sicily.

Women have been in the forefront of protests against French nuclear-testing in the Pacific, while in Japan elderly women built a peace camp at the foot of Mount Fuji to protest against the loss of their Shibokusa homeland to the military, disrupting military exercises and planting scarecrows to decoy the troops. According to one of them, they 'realized that the whole phenomenon of militarism wherever it takes place is violence against the land. So we are really a part of the wider anti-war movement.[8]

An International Peace Festival in the Philippines September 4-17 1991, attended by almost 400 participants from 32 countries, was just being brought to a close when, in a historic vote, the Philippines Senate rejected a military bases treaty which would have extended US presence in the Philippines for a further 10 years. Participants were euphoric. Those in one of the Festival's workshops, on Militarism and Violence against Women, resolved to form a network of Asia-Pacific women for peace, to share information and undertake specific joint actions, particularly on the issue of dismantling foreign military installations and the denuclearization of the region.[9]

In Sri Lanka, where civil war has led to thousands of deaths and the abduction of some 25-60,000 boys and men, seemingly by the People's Liberation Army, an estimated 25,000 women have formed the Mothers Front to protest against the 'disappearance' of their sons and husbands. Although, like the mothers of the 'disappeared' in Argentina and El Salvador, they have received death threats and are accused of subversion, they have held rallies and presented petitions to the government.

It was the non-violent protests, demonstrations and strikes of thousands of Salvadorans, the majority of them women, which were crucial in bringing about a settlement between El Salvador's government troops and the guerrilla forces which had been locked for so long in violent combat.

The killing of three small children in their pram, and the mutilation of their mother, were what triggered the action of the Irish Peace Women. The children's aunt, Mairead Corrigan, expressed such passionate anger and despair on television that women who saw her felt they had had enough. Also in Belfast, Betty Williams expressed her disgust at the tragedy, and invited all women who wanted an end to the war to notify her.

Within less than 48 hours Williams had gathered more than 6,000 signatures to a petition demanding an end to the conflict. She and Corrigan organized a peace march, in August 1976, attended by more than 10,000, a march which took place in total silence. Three months later, 150,000 people in a number of countries had participated in marches to demonstrate their desire for peace in Northern Ireland, in spite of attacks by extremist groups from both of the opposing parties. Corrigan and Williams were awarded the Nobel Peace Prize in 1977.[10]

Welsh women, inspired by the Nordic Women for Peace who had marched from Copenhagen to Paris in the summer of 1981, marched from Cardiff to the Greenham Common Air Force base in August 1981 in protest against Cruise missiles that the government planned to install in 1983. Two years later they were still there, having formed a peace camp using sleeping bags, tepees and caravans. Men came to stay in the camp or visit it, willingly playing a supportive role but remaining in the background; only women from the camp were allowed to talk to the press—a reversal of the usual sex roles. These women made huge personal sacrifices because they felt so strongly about the issue.

Women in Belgrade have been prominent in demonstrations against the Serbian-dominated government's policies and against the violence being perpetrated in the devastating battles between Serbs, Croats and Bosnians which are raining destruction upon the Yugoslav people. Perhaps women, in the depth of their suffering, will be able to bring pressure to bear upon their menfolk to stop the massacre of their families in this sad and war-torn part of the world.

## Women in politics

Although women have as much right as the other 50 per cent of the human race to participate in public policy-making for peace, in which their perspectives and approaches are sorely needed, their actual roles in the political fora where policies are made are well described by Joanne Woodward, chairperson of the US National Women's Conference to Prevent Nuclear War:

> Women were never consulted about the need for 50,000 nuclear warheads, and women have no need to defend the decisions that produced them. Women have no vested interest in protecting or maintaining the *status quo* of military policies because they played no role in developing those policies.

Women in politics have held meetings and published statements with regard to preparations for war, and organized World Women Parliamentarians for Peace in 1985 because of their concern about the arms trade and human survival. And a meeting in Athens in late 1986, organized by Women for a Meaningful Summit, marked a new stage in women's international cooperation for disarmament by bringing their concerns directly to the negotiators themselves, even the heads of state. The meeting was facilitated by Margarita Papandreou, then First Lady of Greece, and the following is an extract from her statement at the meeting on *Women's Role in the International Arena* :

> It became clear to me that the distortion of the economy which is based on the assumption of eventual violent conflict with other nations, other peoples, leaves no chance for achieving goals of social justice, whether for women, for children, minorities or for the impoverished. With the unprecedented threat ... of a nuclear war or a nuclear accident I felt, along with many others, that the women's movement had to join forces with the peace movement and turn its spectacular energies and skills into *changing the war system.* More and more women are realizing that the struggle for women's rights is a larger struggle, a revolutionary struggle, which is inextricably intertwined with peace.

## Writers and researchers

The concepts and insights that women have brought to understanding the economics and the dangers of the arms race demonstrate how urgently women's perspectives are needed in this field. A number of women have made significant contributions to public understanding of the issues and problems involved in disarmament through their writing. One whose contribution to the understanding of the relationship between peace and development has been crucial is Ruth Leger Sivard, whose annual analyses of world military and social expenditures have become indispensable to all concerned with the subject.

In some countries women have been among the most active and productive investigators into the means and possibilities of reducing violence, abolishing war and creating a just and equitable society. They have been members of peace research institutes, university faculties, international organizations, professional associations and other structures through which peace research is conducted, or have founded their own institutes, for example the Institute for Training in Non-Violence set up by Beverly Woodward, the Institute for Defense and Disarmament started by Randall Forsberg, World Priorities founded by Sivard, and the Oxford Research Group established by Scilla Elworthy (at that time Scilla McLean).

Elworthy's books have shed light on the process of nuclear weapons decision-making and the need for public awareness and participation in the process.[11] And in her book *The Game of Disarmament* the late Alva Myrdal, a Swedish arms negotiator and Nobel Peace laureat, writes of the fundamental ineffectiveness of years of negotiation in 'arms talks' which do not reduce arms but simply make some obsolete while opening the way to further development of more sophisticated weapons.[12]

In a Background Paper prepared for a UN Expert Group Meeting on the Participation of Women in Promoting International Peace and Cooperation, which took place in Vienna in December 1983, Dr Elise Boulding of the United States suggested that one strategy for the next women's decade might be to focus upon all the unusual peace-making and peace-keeping skills women have developed, and to campaign to place those skills where they are most needed:

> Three specific targets should be considered: (1) representation of one-third women on all national security bodies and all international security bodies including NATO and the Warsaw Pact;  (2) women's units in the UN Expeditionary Forces; and (3) special UN women's peace brigades for dealing with civil violence. Equivalent national brigades could also be considered.
>
> For the non-governmental sphere, some goals might be: (1) women's encampments at all international borders where violent combat is in process of being threatened, consisting of women trained in non-violence; (2) travelling teams of women mediators sponsored by women's organizations; (3) a special program of recruitment of young women to study international affairs, conflict resolution, and mediation, with scholarship support for such training. Such programs would help make women's contributions to peace-making more visible and accessible.[13]

Women's many significant contributions to disarmament research are recounted by Boulding, one of the world's most distinguished peace researchers, in her paper 'The Role of Women in the Development of Peace Research'.[14] She has suggested the following 'conflict pyramid' to show the various techniques for conflict management:

## THE VIOLENT CONFLICT PYRAMID

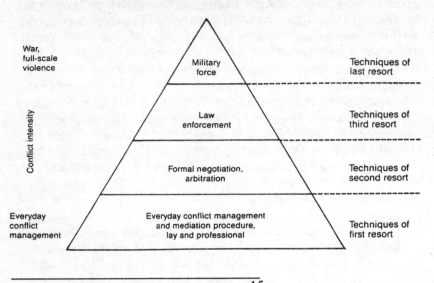

Source:    *Bulletin of the Atomic Scientists* [15]

Yet although women have established, facilitated and contributed to projects providing the basic knowledge we now have about war, militarism, the arms race, and the causes and possible solution to the whole range of global problems, their contributions have often been co-opted or ignored, and only a few women are recognized as leaders in the peace research field, among them Dr Betty Reardon, Director of Peace Research at New York's Columbia University.[16]

The 1983 consultation of women peace researchers at Györ, Hungary, on 'Women, Militarism and Disarmament' identified the following as areas where research is needed:  sexism and sex role socialization; the connections between sexism and other forms of discrimination and violence and between militarism and development;  the common characteristics of feminist and peace movements;  the connections between action and research;  core concepts, root causes and strategies for a change of values and consciousness. Such research was seen as essential to a better understanding of the effects of militarization and the role of women in promoting new and greater awareness of war and peace, and in ensuring that these issues are in the forefront of peace research.

Researchers have also given considerable attention to the understanding of human interaction and social processes as well as to the psychological factors that underlie the arms race; how some of these factors might relate to masculine identity development, and how deeply embedded they are in our culture and behaviour. Some of these factors are revealed in the language of arms development and security analysis. If women's participation and perspectives are badly needed in the policy-making process on issues related to peace, they are equally necessary in producing the knowledge on which such policy is based.

## The feminine approach to problem-solving

The importance of introducing into public affairs those human values which society usually assigns to women, recognized in the Forward-looking Strategies, reflects a recent trend in women's studies. Over the past several years, research into women's way of knowing, reasoning and decision-making has demonstrated that, at least in Western countries, women's thinking tends to be different from that of men, and that this difference can shed new light on—and often produce unprecedented solutions to—some of our major social problems. These modes of thinking and problem-solving can be learned and applied by both men and women.

Research into childhood development, such as that by Carol Gilligan, has shown that young girls, when asked to solve a moral dilemma set in a hypothetical problem, tend to think about and react to the problem differently from boys. They project an 'ethic of care' and see things in terms of relationships, responsibility, caring, context and communication, whereas boys rely on an 'ethic of rights' or 'justice' and analyse problems in abstract terms of right and wrong, fairness, logic, rationality, winners and losers, ignoring context and relationships.[17] While traditional psychological theory has regarded the male type of reasoning as more 'advanced' than the female pattern, feminists have posited an equally valid 'feminine' reasoning based on factors such as non-litigious dispute resolution and non-confrontational negotiation techniques.[18]

Women generally demonstrate a preference for problem-solving through open communication, free access to information, honest discussion of differences and dialogue among all concerned. Their experience of conflict has usually been long and varied, particularly as peace-makers in the family. As mothers, wives and sisters, they are used to resolving disputes and tend to see the best way of doing so as that which helps to meet at least some of the concerns of all conflicting parties— what has come to be called a 'win-win solution', a family model which seeks fairness and reconciliation rather than victory and retribution.

A panel on women and international conflict, convened in Washington in November 1991 with the assistance of the UN Development Programme, took a close look at what women could do to help solve conflict in Northern Ireland, South Africa, Sri Lanka, Jerusalem and Cyprus.[19] Greek Cypriot and Turkish Cypriot panellists described the situation on the island, where UN peace-keeping forces have been stationed since 1963 and which has been divided in two since 1974 as a result of fighting which displaced more than 200,000 people from both communities. There, women professionals are working with men from both sides on a master plan for the divided city of Nicosia, and have set up a centre for women's studies and peace just inside the buffer zone.

In the other countries, too, women are engaged in 'barefoot diplomacy'. Israeli and Palestinian women in Jerusalem, black and white women in South Africa, Catholic and Protestant women in Northern Ireland, and Sinhalese and Tamil women in Sri Lanka, all are engaged in dialogue and are working and campaigning together to achieve peaceful resolution of the problems which have given rise to violent conflict in their countries.

Because of their concern with relationships, women tend toward holistic views which focus on problems in their general context and over a longer time period, including past as well as future. They have special talents as negotiators; in the global context their perspective makes it possible for them to see the inter-relationships between equality, development and peace, and the need to analyse any strategies about each within the context of the other two, and enables them to become catalysts for peace and political change.[20]

1    Washington Irving, 'The Wife', *Sketch Book of Geoffrey Crayon, Gent*, 1819-20.

2    *MS Magazine*, November 1986.

3    See: Elise Boulding, *Women in the 20th Century World*. Sage, New York, 1977.

4    Birgit Brocke-Utne, *Educating for Peace*. Pergamon Press, London, 1985.

5    Elise Boulding, *The Underside of History*, pp.674-5. Westview Press, USA, 1976.

6    Ibid.

7    Researched by Betty Readon for the UN/NGO kit on 'Women and Peace', UN/NGLS Geneva.

8    Quoted by Leonie Caldecott (1983) and in Brock-Utne, op.cit.

9    Asian Women's Human Rights Council, The Philippines. Monograph Series, Vol.1 No.1, 1991.

10   Birgit Brocke-Utne. op.cit.

11   Scilla McLean, ed., *Who Decides? Accountability and Nuclear Decision-making in Britain*. London 1986. Also *How Nuclear Weapons Decisions are Made*, Oxford Research Group, Woodstock, Oxon. OX7 1TE.

12   Alva Myrdal, *The Game of Disarmament*. Pantheon, New York, 1982.

13   Elise Boulding, 'Women's Concepts and Skills, Men's Policies : The Missing Link for Peace', extract from Background Paper on Women's Participation in Decision-Making on Peace, Security and International Co-operation, prepared for Expert Group meeting on the Participation of Women in Promoting International Peace and Cooperation, Vienna, Austria, 5-9/12/83.

14   In *The Role of Women in Peace Movements*. UNESCO, Paris, 1985.

15   Elise Boulding, in 'The Role of Women in the Development of Peace Research.' *Bulletin of Academic Scientists*, 1982. Reproduced in *Educating for Peace*, op.cit.

16   See: Betty Reardon, *Sexism and the War System*. Teachers College Press, New York, 1985.

17   Carol Gilligan, *In a Different Voice: Psychological Theory and Women's Development*. Harvard University Press, Cambridge 1982.

18   Charlesworth, Chinkin and Wright, 'Feminist Approaches to International Law', *American Journal of International Law*, Vol. 85, 1991.

19   On the occasion of the Fifth International Forum of the Association for Women in Development, Washington, Nov. 1991.

20   For part of this chapter I am indebted to research undertaken by Betty Reardon, op.cit.

# 9. WORKING TOWARDS A NON-VIOLENT WORLD

> We have a long, long way to go. So let us
> hasten along the road, the road of human
> tenderness and generosity. Groping, we may
> find one another's hands in the dark.
>
> Emily Greene Balch[1]

As we saw in the last chapter, women can do, and are doing, much to bring about a non-violent world. They are doing so as members of non-governmental organizations, in peace movements, in local communities, as social workers and researchers, in provincial and national politics and in international organizations. Underlying their efforts to prevent or end the outbreak of hositilites and end the arms race has always been an awareness of the political causes of violence and militarism and of the relevance of economic and social justice. Since World War II and the founding of the United Nations, they have arrived at a global perspective on the human condition.

Peace organizations have developed an in-depth analysis of the inter-relationships among world problems, and see their role as helping others to understand the forces of violence that are at the core of most of them.These forces can be, to use Boulding's term, *behavioural violence*, whether personal, domestic, or international violence in the warfare that constantly rips the delicate fabric of human society; or, to use Galtung's phrase, *structural violence*, which destroys the economic and social liberty of individuals and communities; or *institutional violence* as seen under *apartheid*.

While this holistic approach to local and regional actions for peace and justice has always been a pronounced characteristic of peace movements, significant changes are now taking place at the local level throughout the world. Women have become active in debates concerning the major questions of peace, security and international cooperation, and are involved in efforts to ensure implementation of the Nairobi Strategies, which provide a map for future changes to give women their rightful place in social, economic and political life. Principles embodied in international instruments such as the Universal Declaration of Human Rights, international Human Rights covenants, ILO labour standards and the Convention on the Elimination of All Forms of Discrimination Against Women, constitute the case for greater involvement of women in the decision-making process.

Because women's participation in the struggle to achieve a full, just and peaceful world order is so essential, every effort must now be made to increase their effectiveness: by lobbying for implementation of government promises and by increasing the numbers of women in policy-making positions. One of the most important things to be done is to monitor government implementation of the recommendations of the Strategies concerning the modification and acceleration of socio-economic development based on the full and equal participation of women as agents and beneficiaries, and to ensure that national policies and programmes are, or become consistent with, the goals and purposes of the Strategies.

Women should also take more joint action in the area of disarmament. As noted in paragraph 241 of the Strategies, because they 'are still very inadequately represented in national political processes dealing with peace and conflict settlement, it is essential that women support and encourage each other in their initiatives and action relating to disarmament and the development of confidence-building measures between nations and people, or to specific conflict situations between or within States.'

Although their participation in councils which make public policy is so meagre, and even more so in those which make security policy, women are now insisting on being heard, for instance in decisions concerning the conversion of resources from military to civilian purposes, to ensure that women's needs are taken into account.

## Individual and collective rights

Working for a non-violent world means that women must insist upon their right to a full and fair enjoyment of human rights as set forth in the United Nations' Universal Declaration of Human Rights and all of the covenants and conventions intended to protect and implement those rights. They must try to ensure the application of these standards to all relevant situations, to hold governments accountable for their observation and application, and to ensure that individuals and governments are held accountable for their violation. The importance of this point is emphasized in paragraph 13 of the Nairobi Forward-looking Strategies:

> Peace includes not only the absence of war, violence and hostilities at the national and international levels, but also the enjoyment of economic and social justice, equality and the entire range of human rights and fundamental freedoms within society. It ... represents goodwill toward others and promotes respect for life ... Without peace and stability there can be no development. Peace and development are inter-related and mutually reinforcing ...

Thus, the achievement of a world without war means to strive not only for individual rights but also for the collective rights of peoples, especially for the right to development, a healthy environment and a social and international order in which ... rights and freedoms ... can be fully realized.[2] This aim is well expressed in the three inter-related and mutually reinforcing themes of the United Nations Decade for Women: Equality, Development and Peace. These show that working towards a non-violent world means also to work towards the achievement of humane global conditions, and requires a concept of human development based upon the fulfilment of human needs and aspirations and the health of the planet.

The formulation and implementation of such objectives and policies require the full and equitable participation, both as contributors and beneficiaries, of those whose lives are to be affected by the policies. A world at peace can be seen as a social environment favouring the full development of the human being, one characterized at every level, from local to global, by tolerance, mutual respect, and serious attempts to understand and respect differences, so that conflict can be resolved without recourse to violence. This in turn depends upon equity and equality among nations, ethnic groups, and between women and men, as recognized in the Preamble to the United Nations Charter, which reaffirms 'the equal rights of men and women and nations large and small'.

## Political action groups

Women are playing an important role in exercising pressure on governments for the peaceful resolution of conflict. One outstanding example is the committee of Israeli and Palestinian women formed to follow up on a dialogue begun in Brussels in May 1989 at a meeting organized by the Belgian Jewish Secular Cultural Community Centre. That meeting brought Israeli and Jewish women activists, politicians, artists and scholars together with their Palestinian counterparts from the occupied territories and abroad. It culminated in the formulation of seven principles, including the right to self-determination and sovereignty of Palestinians and Israelis; the need to end the occupation and to re-divide the land; the desire of both peoples to live in dignity, freedom and security; the right of each party to choose its representatives to a peace conference; and a commitment to a resolution of the conflict through a negotiated settlement with international guarantees.

The Joint Palestinian/Israeli Women's Co-ordinating Committee was created in June 1989 and has since met regularly. On 10 March 1990 a rally took place in Jerusalem on what was, prior to 1967, no-man's-land, subsequent to a successful petition to the High Court by the Israeli Women's Peace Net for the right to demonstrate in East and West Jerusalem. The following joint statement, signatories to which included major Israeli and Palestinian personalities covering a broad spectrum of political opinions in both communities, received broad coverage in both electronic and written media in Israel:

> We, Palestinian and Israeli women, share a vision of freedom and equality. We are joined in a common struggle against discrimination, oppression and subjugation of any type, be it on the basis of gender, religion or nationality. We declare our commitment to the peaceful resolution of the Israeli-Palestinian conflict and to reconciliation as the ultimate source of liberation for both our peoples. We therefore affirm that each people has the right to live in its own state, within secure and recognized boundaries. It has become clear that in order to achieve this peaceful solution the government of Israel must negotiate with the legitimate representatives of the Palestinian people, the

PLO. The agreement will be based on international guarantees and recognition. From Jerusalem, the city of peace, we call on our sisters everywhere to support our demand.

In December 1990 500 delegates attending the Israeli-Palestinian Women's Peace Conference expressed their alarm and repugnance at the rapid deterioration of conditions in their region: 'We have consistently worked for a just settlement of the Israeli-Palestinian conflict, based on negotiations between the government of Israel and the legitimate representatives of the Palestinian people, the PLO, in order to end occupation and create a Palestinian state side-by-side with Israel'.

Israeli members of the Women's International League for Peace and Freedom (WILPF) participated the following month in a 20,000-strong Human Chain for Peace, joining hands along a 15-mile stretch of highway leading through the mainly Arab-inhabited Wadi Ara in central Israel. Organized by Peace Now, the Union of Arab Mayors and others, it was a strong expression of Arab-Jewish friendship, solidarity and equality in all fields and against plans to settle new Jewish immigrants on confiscated Arab land. Slogans called for an end both to the Iraqi occupation of Kuwait and to the Israeli occupation of the West Bank and Gaza Strip.[3]

The Women's International League for Peace and Freedom has been particularly active with regard to this problem, and has had considerable success in bringing all sides to the conference table. In May 1991 it was instrumental in bringing together in Geneva Israeli and Palestinian women, most of them lawyers, doctors, teachers or otherwise active professionally, to discuss with their European and American counterparts the sort of action which would have to be taken to end the form of *apartheid* which exists in the occupied territories and to arrive at a fair, two-state solution.

WILPF's pioneering role in movements for peace and justice was conspicuously evident in relation to the Gulf War, when women's groups actively campaigned for a negotiated solution. Members of the Iraqi Women's Federation courageously demonstrated for peace before war was declared on 17 January 1991, while the Pan-Arab Women's Solidarity Association called for a resolution of the crisis by Arab nations. An international delegation led by Women for Mutual Security travelled to Baghdad a week before the war to meet with Iraqi women and encourage a peaceful solution. In the US, Churchwomen United delivered over 30,000 peace petition signatures to the White House and Congress, calling for negotiations, not war.

There are many women who are members of international networks working for a non-violent world.[4] But there are also many women who, in their own homes and communities, are working towards the elimination of the violence which pervades society. In their personal relations they practise constructive conflict resolution, and raise their children to resolve their disputes constructively, humanely, non-violently, encouraging cooperation and advocating its emphasis in schools. They discuss the violent images and messages received by children in their everyday lives in an effort to encourage critical reflection of their value and that of alternatives.

As women insist upon freedom from sexual harassment and more harmonious relations in the workplace, they also insist that all workers be treated with dignity. They try to raise consciousness about questions of conflict and disarmament and the peaceful resolution of industrial disputes. Many who are educators of young children try to convey attitudes of respect for others and knowledge of techniques for non-violent conflict resolution. Some who are teachers of older children and in universities are active in the development of peace education and peace studies.

## Education for peace

The United Nations, in its 1978 Declaration on the Preparation of Societies for Life in Peace,[5] called upon all States:

> (i)  To ensure that their policies relevant to the implementation of the present Declaration, including educational processes and teaching methods as well as media information activities, incorporate contents compatible with the task of the preparation for life in peace of entire societies and, in particular, the young generations;
> (ii)  Therefore, to discourage and eliminate incitement to racial hatred, national or other discrimination, injustice or advocacy of violence and war.

In 1985, paragraph 255 of the Nairobi Strategies called for peace education to be established for all members of society,

particularly children and young people: 'Values, such as tolerance, racial and sexual equality, respect for and understanding
of others and good-neighbourliness should be developed, promoted and strengthened'.  Paragraph 256 goes on to say that:

> Women of the world, together with men, should, as in-
> formal educators and socialization agents, play a special
> role in the process of bringing up younger generations in
> an atmosphere of compassion, tolerance, mutual concern
> and trust, with an awareness that all people belong to the
> same world community. Such education should be part of
> all formal and informal educational processes as well as of
> communications, information and mass-media systems.

An Australian peace activist, Nancy Shelley,[6] has suggested
that peace education:

- is concerned with respect for persons, personal relationships, conflict resolution, social justice, sharing the
  world's resources, cooperation and community;
- deals with oppression, sexism, racism, injustice and
  recognizes that violence has to do with power;
- involves a radical approach to curriculum, the structure
  of schools, and the personal relationships within
  schools;
- is concerned for the planet, the environment and the
  connectedness of humans to other life;
- will make a study of war and its causes; will consider
  alternative ways of dealing with conflict, developing the
  machinery for resolving conflict internationally, nationally and personally;
- is not confined to schools but involves the community
  as it moves to affect the whole of society.

Birgit Brock-Utne has said that 'an education for peace is an
education for cooperation, for caring and sharing, for the use of
nonviolence in conflict-solving. An education that fosters competition, conquest, aggression and violence is an education for
war.'[7] She defines peace education as the social process through
which peace is achieved:  the practising of equality of rights and
power-sharing for every member of a given community, the
learning of non-violent conflict resolution skills, and respect for

human rights. She considers disarmament education, development education and human rights education to be integral parts
of peace education.

In her book *A Window onto the Future* Helena Kekkonen,
the well-known Finnish educator,[8] suggests that peace education gives 'the possibility for people to grow in consciousness
of the world's problems, as citizens who work actively on behalf of worldwide positive peace' and adds four more sectors to
those of Brock-Utne: cultural education, environmental education, equality education and moral education.

Educators and researchers like Shelley and Kekkonen,
Boulding, Brock-Utne and Reardon, have made invaluable contributions to the debate concerning the concept and practice of
peace education, and have played a prominent part in its ped-
agogic development. It is natural that women should have been
among the first to recognize the necessity for peace education;
they are fully aware of the fact that, as the first educators of their
children, mothers are in a privileged position to lay the
groundwork for teachers who can later try to influence the ways
in which formal education affects attitudes towards peace-
making and peace-keeping—a difficult task within the average
competitive school system.

Indeed, the role of the mother is of primary importance.
Because it is mainly mothers who care for young children, it is
women who are the fundamental and formative peace educators.
If attitudinal change is the key to achieving a non-violent world,
much of the capacity for achieving it, at least in the long term,
lies in the hands of women. But one of the most important
aspects of non-violence, positive human relationships, comes
from relations of equality and mutual respect between parents.

Education for peace, inevitably based upon cooperative relationships and partnership between men and women, is a lifelong
process which must take place in every learning situation: in the
family, in schools and universities, in local communities, community organizations, places of worship, in the workplace, in
unions, labour and professional organizations, in the halls of
government and diplomacy, in inter-governmental and non-governmental organizations. In short, peace education can and
should be part of every structure and process through which
people and societies learn and conduct their public affairs.[9]

Some mothers, and fathers too, are taking positive steps with
regard to 'parenting for peace'. Involving the entire family in

peace-making activities, they inculcate peaceful and amicable resolution of family conflicts, an ecologically responsible home life which is mindful of the needs of others, and a sense of responsibility for working towards cooperative human rela-tions—in the family, the community and at the global level. In such families there is a conscious effort to develop a sense of justice with regard to the inequities between men and women and between rich and poor people and nations, and to inspire the children to act for change.

This is such a significant arena of peace education that the University for Peace established by the United Nations in 1980 in Costa Rica (a country which has no army) began a pro-gramme on Family Life Education for Peace in 1987. A number of books have been written on the subject, among them one widely admired for its many practical suggestions, written by the parents of four children who made family life an experience in peace education.[10]

## Games, toys and physical punishment

An all too vivid way in which young children learn about war and conflict is through their games and toys. Some women have unthinkingly contributed to the perpetuation of violence by buy-ing toy guns for their children, tolerating the violent types of action portrayed in children's television, and encouraging the young in competitive games and often violent sports.

Parents, teachers and religious leaders, even athletes, have spoken out against the games and toys of violence which are so prominent today. Schools and playgrounds are urged to intro-duce cooperative play which can encourage not only healthy child development but also the acquiring of non-violent attitudes and peaceful behaviour. Alas, while violent games are a source of anxiety to mothers, fathers often feel that such games are good preparation for a tough and competitive masculine world.

The emergence in recent years of outbreaks of uninhibited violence at football games in various countries seems to uphold the theory that the neural systems involved in violence are sensitized and aroused by competitive sport. In a 1971 study to determine what effect competitive sports have on aggressive behaviour, Goldstein and Arms found that hostility significantly increased in persons who had just viewed a football game, but that there was no such increase in people who had observed a gymnastic exhibition.[11] Thus can intense competition lead to catastrophic consequences.

The pervasive availability of war toys makes violence acceptable to very young children. Major conferences have been held to discuss the effect on children's attitudes of toy guns, bombers and tanks, and of peaceful, creative alternatives, and the consequences of advertising such toys have been studied.[12] Women in many countries have protested against the production and sale of war toys; there have been successful campaigns in Norway and Sweden, and in Denmark such playthings have been outlawed.

All over the world movements have been organized against war toys, among them 'Play for Life' in New Zealand, 'Toys for Peace' in the Philippines, and 'Parents for Peaceful Play' in the USA. Brock-Utne tells of mothers who protested, in 1971, when the Aurora Toy Company introduced a new line of torture toys for boys. There were eight different kits, a typical one including a semi-nude female who was to be strapped to the platform of a guillotine with a razor-sharp blade suspended above her throat. The women succeeded in having them withdrawn from the market.[13]

Family violence too can leave an indelible mark on the children who suffer it. In some countries, for example Denmark, the law prohibits physical punishment of children, a painful experience many developmental psychologists believe to increase tendencies toward aggressive behaviour. Many researchers have found that the more violence children experience at the hands of their parents, the more violent they are likely to be as adults, and that the more severely they are punished the more likely they are to become aggressive juvenile delinquents. By subjecting their children to harsh physical punishment parents show how to use force to impose their will on a situation. Such children are likely to be harsh and violent parents, so perpetuating a never-ending cycle of aggressive behaviour.

## Textbooks and the media

The idea of the inevitability of war can be found in many history textbooks, thus contributing to the stereotyping of other cultures and nations and to the reinforcement of the concept of 'the enemy' and of women as inferior to men. Although in recent years teachers have used such textbooks as examples of how *not* to teach history, it is clear that school curricula will have to be updated and most current textbooks replaced if there is to be any possibility of mutual understanding among nations. A number of countries have established special committees responsible for the deletion of stereotyping in textbooks.

But the media, and especially television, carry an even larger part of the blame for the persistence of cultural stereotypes and the negative images of women they so often project. At the same time, the constant barrage of violence on television, so often within reach of the young, has a hugely pernicious effect upon their understanding of ways in which conflicts can be settled. Gun battles and other forms of aggression are daily fare upon our TV sets, which are often used by harried parents as convenient 'babysitters'.

Through programmes such as these, and war-glorifying films such as 'Rambo', the young are assaulted by the ideology that violence must be met by violence and are presented with killers as heroes. Groups in the United States and elsewhere are bringing pressure on TV and film producers to change this constant diet of violence, but there is still a very long way to go before the damage can be brought under control. Even cartoons, both on TV and in the print media, tend to be full of violent situations.

It is now accepted by many researchers that it has been shown, beyond reasonable doubt, that watching television can produce antisocial attitudes and behaviour that would not otherwise occur among entirely normal children.[14] Eysenck and Nias, two British researchers, claimed in 1978 that, on the basis of the many studies which have been made, there is every reason to believe that watching violence on television causes more than one per cent of the population that would otherwise not be violent to resort to violence—which translates, for example, into more than a million Americans.[15]

Laurel Holliday claimed in 1978 that the viewing of television violence was one of the most potent situational factors known to increase aggressiveness,[16] while Leonard Eron, after a 10-year study, concluded in 1974 that the most plausible interpretation of the data was that early viewing of violent television caused later aggression,[17] a reaction found to be more attributable to boys than to girls.

Explanations for this difference, put forward by Holliday, include: that girls are socialized away from aggression and thus prefer less violent television to begin with; that female characters are not as violent as male characters on television and are therefore not as potent role models for aggression; that females are often victims of male violence on television and little girls identify with their pain; and that, possibly, girls watch less television than their brothers because they have to do more housework.[18]

It is not necessary to prove that media violence influences children. Companies would not spend so many millions of dollars if they were not convinced that TV advertising influenced viewers. All television images influence and educate, often in the wrong direction, and children who spend hours every day in front of their television set become desensitized to the use of violence. In media portrayals of violence the emphasis is on the act of aggression, but not on the consequences of that aggression on the victim, thus leading a child to believe that such acts do not lead to suffering, especially if the 'victim' emerges in the next instalment without any sign of injury.

## Teaching conflict resolution

Teaching about alternatives to violence and approaches to cooperation has become an important element of peace education in elementary and secondary schools throughout the world. Teachers of young children and adolescents have developed methods and materials for a wide variety of approaches to teaching conflict resolution, peace-making and the pursuit of justice. Many have worked cooperatively, nationally and internationally, to exchange ideas and support each other's efforts. Different types of NGO are active in the field and able to offer assistance to those seeking to undertake peace education programmes which illustrate the fact that we can only achieve peace through identifying and overcoming the social patterns that reinforce violence and inhibit the achievement of a full partnership between men and women.

For example, the International Peace Research Association's (IPRA) Commission on Peace Education has performed an important role in illuminating the links between women's studies and peace education. Exploring the fundamental causes of war and violence, seeking to develop a form of education to reduce and eliminate them, they have contributed to significant theoretical developments in education for peace.[19]

UNESCO has also played an important initiating and catalytic role in peace education; its 1974 Recommendation on Education for International Cooperation and Peace and Education regarding Human Rights and Fundamental Freedoms, and its 1980 Final Document of the World Congress on Disarmament Education, are two of the most significant documents in the field. They offer a comprehensive view compatible with women's perspectives and reflect the important inter-relationships between security, disarmament, development, human rights and peace. Women peace educators played an important role in formulating both documents.

UNICEF's 1979 kit 'An Approach to Peace Education', published during the International Year of the Child, was intended to be seen as a way of implementing the UNESCO Recommendation. A tool for teachers, its aims were to promote awareness of the problems created by the arms race and the need for disarmament, to foster attitudes of cooperation and tolerance by training pupils in conflict-solving, to deglorify violence on individual, national and international levels, and to create a deeper understanding of the concepts of peace and the necessity for personal involvement in 'building' peace.[20]

As Brock-Utne has pointed out, 'the introduction of peace studies, of courses packed with factual knowledge about the arms race and the dangers of nuclear war, important as they are, may not *change* our modes of thinking. In a Swedish UNESCO report in 1976, no connection was found between the information level of the students and their attitudes to important social questions.' The study concluded that factual information may not change attitudes and modes of thinking if the conditions surrounding the learning situation do not change simultaneously.[21]

True conflict resolution, at the personal, community or state level, presupposes relationships that are based not on the dialectic of domination and obedience but rather on partnership and mutual respect. But it is in the minds of both men and women that changes must be made. This may appear to be easier said than done.

However, in the not so long-term women have an enormously powerful tool with which to achieve a change in social mentality, for the mothers of the world who provide the care of most young children are the first and most formative educators of their children, both male and female. As such, they can inculcate in them, in their early years, genuine respect for others and for the need to solve conflict by tolerance and negotiation, rather than by violence. Men, too, can provide role models for their children, so that they grow up with a full appreciation of the value and equal status of both sexes.

If it is true that the first and most significant setting for education for peace is within the family, it is obvious that harmonious relations between parents—a relationship of equality and mutual respect—is the essential foundation of family and societal peace. Such a relationship is sadly lacking in one-parent families, of which there are increasing numbers. The absence of a father deprives boys of a role model, and allows neither boys nor girls an opportunity to learn from peaceful parental resolution of family problems, quite apart from throwing an extra, and very difficult, educational burden upon the mother.

## Peace camps and congresses

Since 1989 UNICEF has brought some 100,000 children of Lebanon's estranged Muslim and Christian communities together in special peace camps. 'The youngsters arrive at the camps with all the fears, suspicions and hatreds that religious and communal bitterness have bred, some having even taken up arms behind barricades, shooting machine-guns and bazookas at the "other side". When the time comes to leave, however, they take understanding home with them instead of hate, and sometimes—like Fadi (a Maronite Christian) and Daher (a Shiite Muslim)—they part as friends.' [22]

UNICEF started SAWA magazine (the name means 'together') under its Education for Peace project as an alternative educational channel for children unable to attend school because of heavy fighting. It grew to a circulation of 70,000, distributed by non-governmental organizations through dispensaries, clinics and other outlets throughout the country. When SAWA asked its young readers for ideas to remedy the sad situation in Lebanon, they responded overwhelmingly that they needed to come together and get to know each other if they were to learn to live in tolerance, mutual respect and solidarity.

UNICEF's NGO partners helped organize the peace camps, and some 5,000 university-age monitors ran them, having received special training not only in Lebanon's geography and its diverse cultures but in ways to promote ideas of peaceful co-existence and tolerance in their young charges. The camps have succeeded so well that the programme is being introduced in schools as part of the national curriculum.[23]

Many NGO publications have emphasized that boys and girls should be educated in the same fashion so that they become caring, cooperative and responsible members of society. But documents and publications are not the only vehicles for peace education, which can also be practised at the many meetings of various kinds held by NGOs as part of their regular programmes on peace issues. In some cases these events begin with interfaith services to promote mutual respect and tolerance, and children of conference participants are often accommodated in local child-care facilities so that they too experience a multicultural environment.

Among such meetings have been several world congresses organized during the UN Decade for Women by the Women's International Democratic Federation, in cooperation with other international NGOs and national women's committees. One in the Soviet Union brought together over 3,000 peace activists from all over the world, while a session organized by the International Council of Jewish Women in Vancouver in 1987 was devoted to the changing of attitudes, violence in the family and in society, and creating conditions for peace.

Another, organized by the International Council of Women, was held in Malta and dealt with the concept of 'Women, a Force for Peace'. A group called 'Teachers for Peace' has held many seminars on such issues as war toys and school curricula. During the International Year of Peace (1986) many NGOs were given awards as 'Peace Messengers' by the United Nations. Since then, the number of meetings and seminars making the connection between the interlinked subjects of disarmament, development, the environment, and human rights in the interests of a peaceful world has multiplied.

---

1    Emily Greene Balch, b. 1867, US economist and sociologist, first Secretary-General of the Women's International League for Peace and Freedom (WILPF).

2    The Universal Declaration of Human Rights, article 28. United Nations, 1948.

3    WILPF quarterly *Pax et libertas*, March 1991

4    For example, the Feminist Utopian Network, c/o Elise Boulding, Institute for Social Science, University of Colorado, Boulder, Colorado, USA.

5    UN General Assembly, 85th plenary meeting, resolution 33/73 of 15/12/78.

6    Nancy Shelley, 'The case for a feminist contribution to peace education', Australian Women's Education Coalition, October 1982.

7    Birgit Brock-Utne, *Educating for Peace*, p. 72. Pergamon Press, London, 1985.

8    Association of Finnish Adult Education Organizations, Helsinki.

9    Betty Reardon, UN/NGO kit on 'Women and Peace', UN/NGLS, Geneva.

10    James and Kathleen McGinnis, *Parenting for Peace*. Orbis, New York, 1981.

11    In 'Effects of Observing Athletic Contests on Hostility', 1971.

12    Educators for Social Responsibility, 790 Riverside Drive, New York, N.Y.10027.

13    Birgit Brock-Utne, op.cit.

14    See, for example, Liebert, Robert, 'Television and Children's Aggressive Behavior : Another Look', in the *American Journal of Psychoanalysis* 34: 99, 1974.

15    Eysenck, H.J. and Nias, D.K.B., *Sex, Violence and the Media*, 1978.

16    Holliday, Laurel, *The Violent Sex. Male Psychobiology and the Evolution of Consciousness*, 1978.

17    Eron, Leon, in 'How Learning Conditions in Early Childhood— including Mass Media—Relate to Aggression in Late Adolescence'. *American Journal of Orthopsychiatry*. 44:412.

18    Cited in Brock-Utne, op.cit.

19    See esp. the special peace education issue of IPRA's journal, *The Bulletin of Peace Proposals*.

20    Sissel Volan, 'An Approach to Peace Education', UNICEF Development Education kit No.6. United Nations Children's Fund, Geneva, 1979.

21    Birgit Brock-Utne, op.cit..

22    Tuma Hazou, 'Children learn peace in strife-torn Lebanon', in UNICEF quarterly *First Call for Children* No.1, January-March 1992.

23    Ibid.

# 10. MAKING THE CONNECTION

**Not by a radiant jewel, not by the sun nor by fire, but by conciliation alone is dispelled the darkness born of enmity.**

Panchatantra[1]

As we have seen, a non-violent world implies a set of relationships between people, and between nations, based upon trust, cooperation and awareness of the interlinkages between peoples and their mutual interests. It is based upon the recognition that the Earth is a single, interdependent system, with one common future, that all peoples have the same fundamental human needs, are endowed with full human dignity, are entitled to the realization of all human rights, and share a common interest in the future of the planet.

It is now generally accepted that ending discrimination against women and achieving a non-violent world are mutually interdependent, inseparable goals. It is also generally recognized that effective development and an end to structural violence require the full participation of women. The relationship between women's rights, social and economic justice, and non-violent conflict resolution has not only become clearer over the years but is now seen as of the greatest importance to all, not only to women.

## Equal partnerships

In his message to the World Congress of Women in 1987, then-UN Secretary-General Javier Peréz de Cuéllar praised the worldwide contribution of women to the promotión of peace, to social equity and to global development, which he said was becoming increasingly evident:

So, too, is the degree to which women suffer from the persistence of conflict, of hunger and malnutrition, and from the arms race. More than ever, women are becoming active in seeking to overcome these negative phenomena. In this they have demonstrated commitment and determination, standing in the forefront in pursuit of the requirements of a peaceful global society.

Women have brought energy and inspiration to the struggle for social justice and economic progress to the common benefit of all humanity, regardless of sex, race or belief. Unfortunately, women remain inadequately represented at national and international decision-making levels. Where women's views and experience are absent, the political process remains incomplete ...

It must be the mutual goal of governments, intergovernmental and non-governmental organizations, and individuals to act for the preservation of peace, for sustained development and for social justice. The full and equal participation of women in these endeavours is essential.[2]

In his statement on International Women's Day, 8 March 1990, Mr Peréz de Cuéllar went even further:

With each passing day the world is becoming more complex and interdependent. The problems we are facing cannot be resolved by the efforts of only half the population of the globe. Both men and women must work together as equal partners in order to ensure a sustainable future for the generations to come.

Just as the goals of the Charter underlie all the work of the United Nations, so the pursuit of peace has been an integral part of the global effort for the advancement of women. Each of the three World Conferences held during the United Nations Decade for Women (1975-85) has dealt with the issue of peace in relation to the advancement of women.

The World Plan of Action adopted in 1976 by the Mexico City Conference called for 'the full participation of women in all efforts to promote and maintain peace'. The World Conference in Copenhagen in 1980 concluded that progress towards any of the three main objectives of the Decade—equality, development, peace—has a beneficial effect on the others, and consequently that it is only under conditions of peace that it is possible to move forward to the full implementation of the other two objectives of the Decade. In 1985 the World Conference in Nairobi adopted by consensus the Forward-looking Strategies for the Advancement of Women.

## The NGO framework

To support the aims of these conferences non-governmental organizations held a special NGO forum at each of them. In Nairobi the International NGO Women's Forum, for example, included as one of its energetic and colourful components a 'Peace Tent' where women from all over the world exchanged ideas on this issue. During the UN Decade women from different cultures, ideologies and socio-economic backgrounds had unprecedented opportunities to meet together to exchange experiences and to discuss their perceptions of war and peace, of justice and injustice. One of the most positive results has been the development of dialogue between women from all corners of the earth—North and South, East and West—giving rise to a more universal conception of equality, development and peace conducive to better understanding and more harmonious relations among peoples and nations.[3]

As the bearers of human life, women can offer a special perspective and experience which help to overcome prevailing life-destroying methods of dealing with human problems and conflicts. Their approaches to social relations and economic necessity, their concern with harmonious relationships, their skills in maintaining them and in resolving conflicts, reflect capacities which all human beings can develop and which are desperately needed for the survival of human society. Women must make their recognized abilities as peace-makers within the family available at the broader, political level, in the national and international arenas.

Mahatma Gandhi, leader of the non-violent movement against British colonial rule in India, maintained that *only* women were able to save the world from violence, and was convinced that Indian women should take the lead in the civil disobedience (*satyagraha*) movement. Indeed, more than sixty per cent of the participants in the famous Salt March of March 1930 were women, and 17,000 of the 30,000 people arrested were women. The Mahatma considered women more peace-loving than men, and saw that, 'if women were going to play the leading role he wanted them to play, they had to have more power and also fight their own oppression'.[4]

## PROMOTING WOMEN IN CHINESE SOCIETY

Elected chairperson of the Quingdao Women's Federation in 1984, Liu Xiuying found, when trying to promote women to leadership positions in the city government, that few women had been recommended and only a few had applied ... After several months of investigation she and her staff found what appeared to be an invisible net, a social prejudice against women. Women's neglect and frustration came not only from society but from their own sense of inferiority as well. Liu Xiuying began to see the urgent need for the Women's Federation to show society the value of women, and help women become aware of their own value. It was not enough for Chinese women to be independent economically; they must emancipate their minds and spirits as well.

In 1985 the Women's Intellectual Association was formed, with support from the Qingdao Women's Federation. Its 398 members included educators—professors, lecturers, teachers of middle schools, elementary schools and kindergarten—and scientists and technicians, research fellows, engineers, physicians-in-charge and agronomists. A first forum, 'Make Your Career and Your Life a Success", was held in which more than 50 successful women spoke about their experience in coping with their life, their work and their studies ...

Liu Xiuying invited the press to report on the forum, and for several days *Qingdao Daily* and the broadcasting station publicized the achievements of these outstanding women. People throughout the city were inspired, and more than sixty units invited the speakers to give lectures to their members. Even the men were impressed. One commented: 'We never realized that women could show such perseverance in their work. We are surely their inferiors in some ways.'

In 1986 Liu Xiuying organized and became president of the Women's Talent Promoting Association whose aims were to ensure that more women actively participated in politics, and enter the policy-making level, so that women's rights and interests would be considered in the formation and implementation of every policy. All 448 members were government leaders on the county level or above ... they appealed for social support to train more women cadres and to recommend promising candidates to different government agencies.

As a result of Liu Xiuying's work, women's employment in the city rose to 52 per cent in 1986. The Association keeps records on women of ability and recommends candidates to the Municipal Government. Wang Hua, director of Qingdao Agricultural Bank, has offered a core of women ways to improve their self-confidence and their professional skills. As a result more than ten women have become leaders in the bank.

Condensed from *Women of China*, November 1987

If action by women to influence the most important issues of the day is clearly necessary, the ways in which such action can be taken are often only obscurely visualized. The following agenda for action is one in which women, both as individuals and as members of groups, can find relevant ways of making their voices heard on the local and national levels so as to underpin and reinforce efforts which are being made by organizations at the international level. It is important to realize that effective action on the national and global scenes requires, in the first place, information and action at the local level. Every voice, every action, can make a difference.

## An agenda for action

If work at local and national levels to increase awareness of the problems discussed in this book is to be effective it is necessary first to be well-informed, through materials listed in the Bibliography (Annex I) or through information and education materials obtained from the international organizations and non-governmental agencies and groups listed in Annex II. Once informed, there are many ways in which one can participate in this effort.

First, if you have the vote, use it; join a political party, write to your parliamentary or other representative on questions of concern to women. Keep such concerns in mind as you read the newspapers or watch television newscasts about wars and civil disturbances. Monitor them and insist upon balanced reporting. Write letters to the editor, or to the TV programme producer. Join women's groups, church groups or community groups which are mobilizing against militarism, or form one and circulate petitions. Help to organize meetings at which women from the countries in which fighting is taking place will be able to speak about its impact on women. Speak out against racism and intolerance. More specifically:

**At the national level:** remember that the signing of a UN Convention does not guarantee its implementation by the government—this becomes an obligation only after the Convention has been ratified (approved) by the national parliament. If your country has ratified the Convention on the Elimination of All Forms of Discrimination Against Women, research and evaluate measures taken to implement its provisions. How successful

have such measures been? Have they been designed to effectively overcome the constraints against women's participation in
social life and policy-making? If not, find out what can be done
to make the implementation measures as effective as possible.

If your government has signed but not ratified the Convention, or has not even signed it, research the obstacles which
stand in the way of ratification or signature. Determine actions
which you and the groups to which you belong can take on
behalf of ratification. Undertake similar research into your government's implementation of the Forward-looking Strategies.
(These do not require ratification.) Organize a one-day seminar
or symposium on the Strategies for a local NGO, church group
or educational association, or call a meeting of women's groups
and peace groups to plan to cooperate on local implementation of
the measures most relevant to your community.

Make an assessment of national governmental agencies and
officials who have the capacity to undertake some of the implementation measures, identifying those who could act on particular measures, and start a campaign to approach them with suggestions for cooperation and how your group might facilitate
their task.

Challenge the legal system, and make it work for women.
Sensitize police, lawyers and judges to women's issues. Help to
make legal services accessible to women, and fight discriminatory and unjust laws and practices that are unfair to women.
The gap between laws that are on the statute books and laws that
actually affect women's lives is often a glaring one, and attempts
to bridge it are often hampered by the idea that the legal system
is beyond the reach of 'ordinary' people. Legal jargon, the
highly formalized practice of law, and the cost of legal action are
often a major stumbling block. Women's groups in some
countries have tried to 'demystify the law' by informing women
of their legal rights and translating jargon and procedures into
plain language so as to make the law work for them.

Researching the numbers of women parliamentarians and of
women with particular responsibilities in your Foreign Ministry,
in your United Nations delegation, on the foreign affairs and
national security committees of your legislature and national executive administration, can be quite an eye-opener. How have
those concerned achieved their positions? Are their policy
orientations different from those of men? Are they prepared to
promote the equality of women? Were they supported by

# DEMYSTIFYING THE LAW
## Strategies for Action

### How Can We Become More Legally Literate?

Source:    *The Tribune*, Newsletter 45.[5]

women for their posts? How many women participate in the security policy-making process in your country? How can women have more influence on peace and security policies?

Take a look at the needs of women and young children which are not being met for lack of funds, and find equivalent amounts in the military budget for items you believe to be unnecessary for security. Tables and charts showing these relationships can be presented to women's groups and organizations for discussion. Look into what some of these NGOs are doing to improve the situation, and how you can help them.

If plans for economic conversion exist, identify which are most likely to be successful, and how they will affect women. Try to inform the public and local and national officials about these possibilities. If your country has a governmental agency working on conversion, find out what it does and what plans it has made; if not, find out how one could be established. Look into government plans for alternative security systems, disarmament and international peace-keeping, and what it intends to do with any 'peace dividend'.

Seek interviews with office holders who might be persuaded to think in fresh terms about peace and security issues, and assemble a list of policy analysts (both men and women) aware of interlinkages between disarmament and women's issues. Help those who organize media campaigns to have more women conscious of these issues appointed or elected to security policy-making positions. Petition your national delegates to the European 'security clubs' (see Chapter 5) and United Nations meetings on disarmament.

**At the local level:**   plan ways to inform the public about these and other initiatives, and organize women to express their support for them, for example through a symposium on Women's Peace and Security Policy. Invite people of varying views to present their concepts of criteria for women's approaches to peace and security, and see how these would differ from present policies and goals.

Organize a workshop for local educators on the UN Decade for Women and use the event to encourage and facilitate teaching about these issues. Check library indices, bibliographies, research journals and other up-to-date sources for writings on peace and security questions. How many women writers do you find? Of these, how many offer analyses and proposals different from those of male analysts?

Find out whether schools and universities in your community offer lessons, units or courses in education for peace and non-violence. If so, see how successful they are and whether they might be used to help educate the general public. If not, encourage authorities to introduce such studies and to emphasize the peaceful resolution of conflicts both at home and at school.

Organize, or help to organize, a peace education fair in your community, with displays of books, lesson plans and educational materials. Try to get materials from other countries to include in the display. Show films and audio-visual learning materials, and have teachers present demonstration lessons. Design a media education programme and encourage its implementation by journalists, scriptwriters, television producers, etc.

Matthew Arnold (1822-88) said: 'If ever the world sees a time when women shall come together purely and simply for the benefit of mankind, it will be a power such as the world has never known.' And in 1910 Hypatia Bradlaugh Bonner saw that the movement would grow:

> If some women are on the side of peace today, more will be tomorrow, for as they get deeper and wider insight into national and international affairs so will they come to see that their whole interests are opposed to militarism and bound up with the maintenance of peace.[6]

Women, after all, are at least half of humanity. They can work miracles by setting an example, and by insisting upon realization of the promise contained in the Preamble to the Universal Declaration of Human Rights:

> *Whereas* recognition of the inherent dignity and of the equal and inalienable rights of all members of the human family is the foundation of freedom, justice and peace in the world ... the peoples of the United Nations have in the Charter reaffirmed their faith in fundamental human rights, in the dignity and worth of the human person and in the equal rights of men and women, and have determined to promote social progress and better standards of life in larger freedom...

1    c. 5th C, in a translation by Franklin Edgerton.

2    As reported in *Women of the Whole World*, Journal No.3, 1987.

3    'World Problems and Human Potential', *Transnational Associations* No.4, July/August 1986.

4    Birgit Brocke-Utne, *Educating for Peace*, Pergamon Press, London, 1985.

5    *Women and Law*, July 1990. International Women's Tribune Centre, 777 United Nations Plaza, New York, NY 10017.

6    Quoted in the WILPF Newsletter of the *Women versus Violence Project*, Vol.1, No.1, October 1990. Women's International League for Peace and Freedom, 1 rue de Varembé, CP 28, 1211 Geneva 20.

## SELECTED BIBLIOGRAPHY

Alderson, Lynn, 'Greenham Common and All That', in *Breaching the Peace*. Only Women Press Ltd., London, 1983.

Amnesty International, *Women in the Front Line*. 322 Eighth Avenue, New York, NY 10001, December 1990.

Anderson, Marion, *Neither Jobs nor Security: Women's Unemployment and the Pentagon Budget*. Employment Research Associates, Lansing, MI, 1982.

Arcana, Judith, *Every Mother's Son. The role of mothers in the making of men*. The Women's Press, London, 1983.

Ballara, Marcela, *Women and Literacy*. Zed Books, London, 1992.

Berezhnaya and Blinova, *Women fight for peace*. Moscow, Scientific Research Council on Peace and Disarmament, 1986.

Bhushan, Madhu, *Women and Violence*. Sangharsh, India, 1986.

Boulding, Elise,*Women in the 20th Century World*. Sage, New York, 1977.
- 'The Role of Women in the Development of Peace Research'. *Bulletin of the Atomic Scientists*, 1982.
- 'Mutual relationships between women's status in society and the building of peace'. Paper prepared for UN Expert Group Meeting in Vienna, December 1983 .
- 'Women's Participation in decision-making on peace, security and international cooperation'. Paper prepared for Expert Group Meeting in Vienna, December 1983.
- 'Women's Concepts and Skills, Men's Policies : The Missing Link for Peace'. Background paper on Women's participation in decision-making on Peace, Security and International Cooperation, prepared for Expert Group Meeting, Vienna, December 1983.

Boylan, Esther, *Women and Disability*. Zed Books, London, 1991.

Brock-Utne, Birgit, *Education for Peace: a feminist perspective*. Pergamon Press, London/New York, 1985.
- 'The Role of Women as Mothers and Members of Society in the Education of Young People for Peace, Mutual Understanding and Respect for Human Rights.' Paper for UNESCO expert meeting on the role of women in peace education. New Delhi, 1981.
- 'Feminist perspectives in peace research'. In *PRIO Report*, International Peace Research Institute, Oslo, 1986.

Bunch, Charlotte and Carillo, Roxanna, *Gender Violence: A Development and Human Rights Issue*. Commonwealth Secretariat, London, 1988.

Connors, Jane Frances, *Violence against women in the family*. United Nations, Vienna, 1989.

Caldicott, Helen, *Missile Envy: The Arms Race and Nuclear War*. Bantam Books, 666 Fifth Avenue, New York, NY 10016, 1986.

Commission of the Churches on International Affairs, *Disarmament Prospects and Problems*, World Council of Churches, 150 Route de Ferney, Geneva, 1990/2.

Deonna, Laurence, *The War with Two Voices*. Three Continents Press, Washington D.C., 1989.

Ehrenreich, Barbara, and Fuentes, Annette. *Women in the global factory*. South End Press, New York, 1983.

Eisler, Riane, *The Chalice and the Blade*. Harper & Row, New York, 1987.

El-Saadwi, Nawal, *The Hidden Face of Eve: Women in the Arab World*. Zed Press, London, 1980; and Beacon Press, Boston, 1982.

Elshtain, Jean B, *Women and War*. Basic Books, New York 1987.

Elworthy (ex-McLean) Scilla (ed.), *Who decides? Accountability and nuclear decision-making in Britain*. London, 1986.
-  *How nuclear weapons decisions are made*, Oxford Research Group, Woodstock, Oxon. PX7 1TE.
-  'The role of women in the promotion of friendly relations between nations', in *The Role of Women in Peace Movements*. UNESCO, Paris, 1980.

Enloe, Cynthia, *Does Khaki Become You? The Militarisation of Women's Lives*. Pluto Press, London, 1983.

Eron, Leonard, *et al*. 'How Learning Conditions in Early Childhood—including Mass Media—Relate to Aggression in Late Adolescence'. *American Journal of Orthopsychiatry*, 44, 1974.

Eysenck, H.J. and Nias, D.K.B., *Sex, Violence and the Media*. Maurice Temple Smith, London, 1978.

Florence, Mary Sargent, Catherine Marshall and C-K. Ogden, *Militarism versus Feminism, Writings on Women and War*. Virago Press, 41 William IV Street, London WC2N 4DB, 1987.

Forbes Martin, Susan, *Refugee Women*. Zed Books, London, 1992.

Gandhi, Mahatma, 'What is Women's Role?' *Harijan* 24, 1940.

Gilligan, Carol, *In a Different Voice*. Harvard University Press, Cambridge, 1981.

Goldstein, Jeffrey, and Arms, Robert, 'Effects of Observing Athletic Contests on Hostility'. *Sociometry* No.34, 1971.

Heikens, Carolein, 'Freedom Fighters', in *Loaded Questions. Women in the Military*. Transnational Institute, Amsterdam and Washington DC, 1981.

Holliday, Laurel, *The Violent Sex. Male Psychobiology and the Evolution of Consciousness*. Bluestocking Books, Guerneville, CA, 1978.

International Labour Organization:
-  Ball, N., 'Converting the workforce: defence industry conversion in the industrialized countries'. International Labour Review Vol.125, No.4, July/August 1986.
-  Engelgardt, K., 'Employment effects of disarmament on research and development personnel'. ILR Vol.124.

- Thee, M., 'Swords into ploughshares: the quest for peace and human development'. ILR Vol. 122, Sept./ Oct. 1983.

Jolly, Richard (ed.), *Disarmament and Development*. Pergamon Press, Oxford, 1978.

Jones, Lynne (ed.), *Keeping the Peace. Women's Peace Handbook*. The Women's Press, London, 1983.

Kiranova, Evgenia, *In the Year of Peace - a story of the Bulgarian peace movement*. Sofia, 1986.

Mansueto, Connie, 'Take the Toys from the Boys. Competition and the Nuclear Arms Race', in *Over Our Dead Bodies*. Virago Press, London, 1983.

McGinnis, James and Kathleen, *Parenting for Peace*. Orbis, New York, 1981.

McLean, Scilla, see Elworthy.

Mische, Gerald, 'The Feminine and World Order", *Breakthrough*, Fall 1986.

Myrdal, Alva, *The Game of Disarmament*. Pantheon, New York, 1982.

Pietilä, Hillka and Vickers, Jeanne, *Making Women Matter: The Role of the United Nations*. Zed Books, London, 1990.

Pines, Susan, 'Women's Pentagon Action', in *My Countries in the Whole World. An Anthology of Women's Work on Peace and War*, Cambridge Women's Peace Collective. Pandora Press, London, Boston, Melbourne, 1984.

Reardon, Betty, *Sexism and the War System*. Teachers College Press, New York, 1985.
  - *Militarization, security and peace education: a guide for concerned citizens*. Valley Forge, United Ministries in Education, 1982.
  - *Education for global responsibility: a guide to teacher-designed peace education curriculum*. Teachers College Press, New York, 1988.

Rodda, Annabel, *Women and the Environment*. Zed Books, London, 1991.

Schuler, Margaret (ed.) *Empowerment and the Law: Strategies of Third World Women*. OEF International, 1815 H.St. NW, Washington DC 20006, 1985.

Shelley, Nancy, 'The case for a feminist contribution to peace education', Australian Women's Education Coalition, October 1982.

Sivard, Ruth Leger, *Women ... a world survey*. World Priorities, Box 25140, Washington DC 20007, 1985.
  - *World Military and Social Expenditures 1991*, World Priorities, as above.

Smyke, Patricia, *Women and Health*. Zed Books, London, 1991.

Steinmetz, Suzanne K. and Strauss, Murray A. (eds.), *Violence in the Family*. Dodd, Mead, New York, 1974.

UNESCO, International Expert Meeting on the Role of Women in the Education of Young People for Peace, Mutual Understanding and Respect for Human Rights. Paris, December 1981 (Ed/82/Conf.609/ Col.3).

-   The role of women in peace movements, in the development of peace research, and in the promotion of friendly relations between nations. 1980.
-   International Meeting of Experts on factors influencing women's access to decision-making roles in political, economic and scientific life, and on measures that may be taken to increase their responsibilies. Paris, 1985. (SH3-84/Conf.601/5).

United Nations: Report of Expert Group Meeting on the Participation of Women in Promoting International Peace and Cooperation. UNDAW, Vienna, 5-9 December 1983.
-   Annotated Bibliography of Women/Peace Questions since 1975. Expert Group Meeting, Vienna, December 1983. UNDAW, November 1983
-   World Survey on the Role of Women in Development, Update. UNDAW, 1987.
-   Report of the World Conference to Review and Appraise the Achievements of the United Nations Decade for Women: Equality, Development and Peace, Nairobi, 15-26 July 1985.
-   Report of the Secretary-General on Implementation. Vienna, 2 September 1987, (A/42/516).
-   Final Document of the 1978 Special Session of the General Assembly devoted to Disarmament. New York, 1978.
-   *Refugee Women and International Protection.* UNHCR, Geneva, 1985.
-   *The World's Women 1970-1990.* UN Statistical Office, New York.
-   UN/NGO Group on Women and Development with Zed Books, London, series on Women and World Development.

Vargas, Ines, *Women and Violence.* International Peace Research Institute, Oslo, Working Paper 17/83.

Vickers, Jeanne, *Women and the World Economic Crisis.* Zed Books, London, 1991.

Volan, Sissel, *An Approach to Peace Education.* UNICEF, Geneva, 1979.

## ACRONYMS AND ABBREVIATIONS

**AAWORD:**   Association of African Women for Research and Development

**CEDAW**   Committee on the Elimination of Discrimination against Women (UN)

**CIA**   Central Intelligence Agency (United States)

**CIS**   Commonwealth of Independent States

**C of E**   Council of Europe

**CSCE**   Conference on Security and Cooperation in Europe

**DAWN**   Development Alternatives with Women for a New Era

**GDP**   Gross domestic product

**GNP**   Gross national product

**IAEA**   International Atomic Energy Agency (UN)

**ILO**   International Labour Organization (Office)

**IMF**   International Monetary Fund

**IPAC**   [Women's] International Policy Action Committee

**IPPNW**   International Physicians for the Prevention of Nuclear War

**IPRA**   International Peace Research Association

**IPU**   Inter-Parliamentary Union

**LDCs**   Least developed countries

**NAA**   North Atlantic Assembly

**NASA**   National Aeronautics and Space Administration (US)

**NATO**   North Atlantic Treaty Organization

**NGO**   Non-governmental organization

**NOAA**   National Oceanographic and Atmospheric Administration (US)

**NPT**   Treaty on Non-Proliferation of Nuclear Weapons

**OPEC**   Organization of Petroleum Exporting Countries

**PLO**   Palestine Liberation Organization

**UNCED**   United Nations Conference on Environment and Development

**UNDP**   United Nations Development Programme

| | |
|---|---|
| **UNESCO** | United Nations Educational, Scientific and Cultural Organization |
| **UNHCR** | United Nations High Commissioner for Refugees |
| **UNICEF** | United Nations Children's Fund |
| **UNRWA** | United Nations Relief and Works Agency for Palestinian Refugees |
| **WAND** | Women and Development |
| **WEDO** | Women's Environment and Development Organization |
| **WEU** | Western European Union |
| **WIDF** | Women's International Democratic Federation |
| **WILPF** | Women's International League for Peace and Freedom |
| **WMS** | Women for Mutual Security |
| **YWCA** | Young Women's Christian Association |

# INSTRUMENTS AND INTERNAL AGENCIES DEALING WITH QUESTIONS OF PEACE, SECURITY AND WOMEN IN DEVELOPMENT

## A: Relevant United Nations Instruments

Preamble and Articles 1 and 2 of the United Nations Charter, 1945.

Universal Declaration of Human Rights, proclaimed by General Assembly (GA) resolution 217 A (III) of 10 December 1948.

Convention on the Political Rights of Women, adopted by GA resolution 640 (VII) of 20 December 1952, entered into force 7 July 1954.

International Covenant on Economic, Social and Cultural Rights, adopted by GA resolution 2200 A (XXI) of 16 December 1966, entered into force 3 January 1976.

International Covenant on Civil and Political Rights, adopted by GA resolution 2200 A (XXI) of 16 December 1966, entered into force 23 March 1976.

Declaration on the Promotion among Youth of the Ideals of Peace, Mutual Respect and Understanding between Peoples, proclaimed by GA resolution 2037 (XX) of 7 December 1965.

Declaration on the Elimination of Discrimination against Women, proclaimed by GA resolution 2263 (XXII) of 7 November 1967.

Declaration on Social Progress and Development, proclaimed by GA resolution 2542 (XXIV) of 11 December 1969.

Universal Declaration on the Eradication of Hunger and Malnutrition, adopted on 16 November 1974 by the World Food Conference convened under GA resolution 3180 (XXVIII) of 17 December 1973, and endorsed by GA resolution 3348 (XXIX) of 17 December 1974.

Declaration on the Protection of Women and Children in Emergency and Armed Conflict in the struggle for peace, self-determination, national liberation and independence, proclaimed by General Assembly resolution 1861 (LVI) of 16 May 1974, and endorsed by GA resolution 3318 (XXIX) of 14 December 1974.

Declaration on the Use of Scientific and Technological Progress in the Interests of Peace and for the Benefit of Mankind, proclaimed by GA resolution 3384 (XXX) of 10 November 1975.

Declaration on Fundamental Principles concerning the Contribution of the Mass Media to Strengthening Peace and International Understanding, to the Promotion of Human Rights and to Countering Racialism, *Apartheid* and Incitement to War, proclaimed by the General Conference of UNESCO, 28 November 1978.

Declaration on the Preparation of Societies for Life in Peace, 1978.

Convention on the Elimination of All Forms of Discrimination against Women, adopted by GA resolution 34/180 of 18 December 1979, entered into force 3 September 1981.

Declaration on the Right of Peoples to Peace, approved by GA resolution 39/11 of 12 November 1984.

Declaration on the Right to Development, adopted by GA resolution 41/128 of 4 December 1986.

Declaration on the Participation of Women in Promoting International Peace and Cooperation, proclaimed 3 December 1982.

## B: United Nations (including specialized agencies and voluntary programmes and funds):[1]

UN Centre for Social Development and Humanitarian Affairs (Division for the Advancement of Women, UNOV/VIC, PO Box 500, A-1400 Vienna).[2]

UN Children's Fund (UNICEF), New York/Geneva.

UN Commission on the Status of Women, and

UN Committee on the Elimination of Discrimination against Women, New York/Vienna.

UN Development Fund for Women (UNIFEM, UNDP), Room FF-1120, 304 East 45th Street, New York.

UN Development Programme (UNDP), New York.

UN Educational, Scientific and Cultural Organization (UNESCO), 7 Place de Fontenoy, F.75007, Paris.

UN Environment Programme, Nairobi, Kenya.

UN Food & Agriculture Organization (FAO), Rome.

UN Fund for Population Activities, UN New York.

UN High Commissioner for Refugees (UNHCR), Palais des Nations, Geneva.

UN Institute for Disarmament Research, Room A-210, Palais des Nations, Geneva.

UN Non-Governmental Liaison Service, Joint UN/NGO Group on Women and Development, Palais des Nations, CH-1211 Geneva 10.[3]

UN Research and Training Institute for the Advancement of Women, P.O.Box 21747, Santo Domingo, Dominican Republic.

International Fund for Agricultural Activities, Via del Serafico 107, 00142 Rome.

International Labour Organization, Women Workers Office, 4 route des Morillons, CH-1211 Geneva 22.

World Bank/International Finance Corporation, 1818 H. Street N.W., Washington DC 20433.

World Food Programme, Via delle Terme di Caracalla, 00100 Rome.

World Health Organization, 20 Avenue Appia, 1211 Geneva 27.

## C.  Non-Governmental  Organizations:

Association of African Women for Research & Development (AAWORD), c/o CODESRIA, BP 3304, Dakar.

Baha'i International Community, CP 433, CH-1290, Versoix, Geneva.

Development Alternatives with Women for a New Era (DAWN), APDEC, Pesiaran Duta, PO Box 12224, Kuala Lumpur.

International Alliance of Women, Alemannengasse 42, CH-4058 Basel.

International Center for Research on Women, 1717 Massachusetts Avenue, NW, Washington DC 20036.

International Coalition for Development Action (ICDA), 22 rue des Bollandistes, 1040 Brussels.

International Council of Jewish Women, 1 rue de Varembé, CH-1202 Geneva.

International Council of Women, 18 bis Montchoisis, CH-1006 Lausanne.

International Council on Social Welfare, 50 Grand Montfleury, CH-1290 Versoix.

International Federation of Women in Legal Careers, 15 Avenue Dapples, CH-1006 Lausanne.

International Federation of Women Lawyers, 42 rue de Vermont, CH-1202 Geneva.

International Federation of University Women, 30 Avenue Krieg, CH-1208 Geneva.

Medical Women's International Association, 34 chemin Pont-Céard, CH-1290 Versoix.

Soroptimist International, Batelière 2, CH-1007 Lausanne.

Third World Network, 87 Cantonment Road, 10250 Penang, Malaysia.

Women's International Democratic Federation, Unter den Linden 143, 1080 Berlin.

Women's International Information & Communication Service, CP 2471, CH-1211 Geneva 20

Women's International League for Peace and Freedom, 1 rue de Varembé, CH-1211 Geneva.

World Association of Girl Guides & Girl Scouts, Les Fossées, CH-1248 Hermance.

World Federation of Methodist Women, 103bis Route de Thonon, CH-1222 Vésenaz, GE.

World Movement of Mothers, 13 ch. du Nantet, CH-1245 Collonge-Bellerive.

World University Service, 5 ch. des Iris, CH-1216 Cointrin, Geneva.

World Union of Catholic Women's Organizations, 'La Châtaigneraie", CH-1297 Founex.

World Young Women's Christian Association, 37 Quai Wilson, CH-1201 Geneva.

Zonta International, 22 Ave. du Château, CH-1008 Prilly, Switzerland.

1    Many of the organizations listed in **B** and **C** contributed to the preparation of the joint UN/NGO development education kit on 'Women and Peace'.

2    CSDHA/DAW, United Nations, Vienna, was the substantive secretariat and focal point for the 'Women and Peace' kit.

3    Under the aegis of the Joint United Nations Information Committee (JUNIC), UN/NGLS is now the substantive secretariat for the UN/NGO Group on Women and Development, whose main activity is the preparation of the book series "Women and World Development" for publication by Zed Books, London.

# EDUCATION GUIDE

This annex is intended to provide assistance to those wishing to use the book for teaching or discussion purposes. It includes information on how to organize a discussion group, seminar or workshop, and a guide for the discussion leader.

## How to organize a discussion group, seminar or workshop

Those who plan the seminar, and group leaders, should be well chosen, well prepared for their tasks and should get to know each other, their backgrounds and their main interests. They should discuss the different aspects of the subject in order to clarify issues and concepts, as well as controversial points which might slow down the process. Responsibility for each aspect of the preparatory work should be defined, including plans for evaluation and follow-up.

**First Session:** Ask the members of the group to introduce themselves briefly, indicating their motivation for joining the group. Test the level of awareness by asking everyone to take a piece of paper and note the six characteristics which first come to mind when they think of women and war. If possible, show a relevant video, then introduce the topic to the group. Open the floor for discussion, making sure that each expresses his or her expectations from the group meeting. If the group exceeds 10 or 12 persons, subdivide it or ask pairs to exchange ideas for 10 minutes prior to group discussion. Each session should last for approximately 90 minutes. If possible, invite a resource person to address this and/or the final session.

**Subsequent Sessions:** Taking the various chapters, introduce the issues raised therein to the group or ask someone who is well-prepared to do so. If possible, make a copy of the chapter for everyone. Guide the discussion on the basis of the questions suggested in the discussion guide (pp.172-174). Do not hesitate to make up your own questions. Where relevant, the group could use 20 minutes for preparing a role-play on one of the situations examined in the book (e.g. the Gulf War).

**Final Session:** Discuss a possible plan of action for your community. Identify the aspects of major interest upon which your group can concentrate its activities. Invite parliamentarians and local authority officials prepared to cooperate, and representatives of peace research institutes and of non-governmental organizations concerned with issues relating to women and war (e.g. United Nations Associations, UNICEF national committees, Women's International League for Peace and Freedom). Identify short-term and long-range goals. Ensure that each member of the group understands his/her possibilities for action. Set a date for the first progress report.

## Suggested check-list for the preparatory meeting

* Introduction of participants.
\* General debate on the subject; clarification of issues and concepts.
* Objectives, target groups, and intended results of the seminar.
* Criteria upon which participants should be selected.
* Identification of resource persons.
* Cooperation with other local and international groups.
* Language(s) in which the seminar will be conducted.
* Decisions on place and date of seminar, and registration fee.
* Organization of schedule (see below) and method of work.
* Responsibility for each aspect of preparatory work to be clearly defined; selection of preparatory and homework materials.
* Decisions concerning distribution of programme announcements (six weeks prior to event, through co-sponsoring groups).
* Design of evaluation sheet to be distributed to participants.
* Plans for follow-up activities.

## HOW TO USE THE BOOK FOR A SEMINAR OR WORKSHOP

The schedule on the following page is based upon the themes contained in *Women and War*, and presupposes a minimum of five days and a group not exceeding 35 participants. Should there be more or less time, or a different number of participants, the programme can be modified. For example, a workshop to take place at the local level could be spread over several weeks, with one-day or evening sessions dealing with specific aspects and topics.

Working groups should have no more than 10-15 participants, including a moderator and rapporteur. Brief reports on the main conclusions of working group discussions should be submitted to plenary sessions, and the Final Report should be based upon them and upon the plenary discussions.

Participants can be asked to list situations which they consider relevant, and invited to suggest posters which could transmit succinct and effective messages to the general public. Inviting talented participants to chair a working group can contribute to their leadership development, but the chairing of the last session, including summing-up, presentation and adoption of recommendations, should be by an experienced person.

The following questions, which relate to the different chapters, are of varying degrees of difficulty. Discussion leaders can choose among them, depending upon the age and state of knowledge of the group, amend them in order to meet the needs of the group concerned, or provide questions of their own. They should ask participants to state the goals and concerns they bring to the study group, and suggest a list of common learning targets which may be generally useful to the whole group.

| SEMINAR | First day | Second Day | Third Day | Fourth day | Fifth day |
|---|---|---|---|---|---|
| 09.00-10.30 | - | Introduction to the subject Lecture and discussion | Militarism and Militarization. Lecture and discussion | Human Rights and Global Security Lecture and discussion | Presentation of working group reports: Plenary |
| 10.30-11.00 | - | (coffee/tea) | (coffee/tea) | (coffee/tea) | (coffee/tea) |
| 11.00-12.30 | - | Impact of War on women: Panel discussion | Working groups on above topic (written reports) | Working groups on above topic (written reports) | Preparation of Plan of Action |
| 12.30 | | (Lunch) | (Lunch) | (Lunch) | (Lunch) |
| 14.30 | Arrival of participants, registration | The Causes of Conflict Lecture and discussion | Defining Security Panel discussion | Women's Visibility; Making the Connection Panel discussion | Plenary: Presentation and adoption of Plan of Action |
| 16.30-1700 | (coffee/tea) | (coffee/tea) | (coffee/tea) | (coffee/tea) | (coffee/tea) |
| 17.00 | Welcoming addresses & introduction of participants | Working groups on above topics (written reports) | Working groups on above topic (written reports) | Working groups on above topic (written reports) | Closure of seminar |
| 18.30 | Films, exhibits | (continued) | (continued) | (continued) | |
| 19.30 | (Dinner) | (Dinner) | (Dinner) | (Dinner) | |

## Discussion guide

### Chapter I : An introduction to the war game

1. Given the end of military competition between the United States and the former Soviet Union, how do you see the possibilities for achieving a peaceful world during the last decade of the 20th century?
2. Do you think that ethnic tensions and nationalist desires for independence will delay the peace process? Explain.
3. What effect do high expenditures on arms have on the social and economic structures of developing countries?
4. Why is nuclear proliferation considered to be the greatest danger facing the world today? Who is responsible for it? What can be done to counter it?
5. What is the role of the United Nations in efforts to reduce violence between and within nations?

### Chapter 2 : The impact of war on women

1. Do educational systems and military training systems engender a respect for women's human rights, both in general and in times of war?
2. Why are women particularly vulnerable in conditions of war or civil strife? What forms of personal violence against women are prevalent in wartime?
3. Why do women and children constitute at least 80 per cent of the world's refugee population? Why is the situation of refugee women particularly precarious?
4. What is the situation of women under *apartheid* ? Which countries have or have had such régimes? Try to imagine what it is like to live under conditions of *apartheid* and how it would influence your outlook on peace and conflict in society.
5. What measures have been taken by the United Nations system to protect the vulnerable in time of war?

### Chapter 3 : The causes of conflict

1. Why do wars erupt? What are the basic causes of conflict?
2. What is meant by 'militarism' and 'militarization'?
3. What can be done to reduce defence budgets? Why have these grown so rapidly in the developing world?
4. What role have women played in the growth of militarism?
5. What is the connection between military spending and maldevelopment?

## Chapter 4 : Lessons of the Gulf War

1. What was the action by Iraq which triggered the Gulf War? What were the reasons for that action?
2. What measures were taken by the United Nations to induce Iraq to withdraw? Do you believe that, with time, UN sanctions would have been effective?
3. Why did the Security Council decide to unleash an 'unlimited' war upon Iraq? Did this achieve its objective?
4. What were the social and economic costs of that war upon Iraq, and upon the region as a whole?
5. Who were the victims? Is the Gulf War likely to have improved the situation of women in Kuwait and Saudi Arabia?

## Chapter 5 : What constitutes security?

1. What are the human costs of a concept of security which gives priority to the perception of military threat?
2. What is the significance of Ruth Leger Sivard's analyses of the human, economic and social costs of expenditures on armaments? What is the impact of military production and activity on the global environment?
3. Do you consider that economic conversion, from war production to civilian purposes, would lower the threshhold of violence? Will it create unemployment, or lead to increased and more useful employment?
4. What is the relationship between disarmament and development? What is the 'peace dividend', and how should one be used?
5. Which European 'security clubs' are involved with keeping the peace? How do you see the prospects for European and UN intervention measures to impose cessation of hostilities?

## Chapter 6 : Human rights and global security

1. It is said that the concept of human rights is the foundation of peace, and that peace is a human right. Comment, explaining how you might articulate a vision of global security based upon economic and social justice and non-violence.
2. Basic human rights are said to include the right to food, health and education. How well are these basic rights observed in practice, so far as women are concerned? Why is it said that the condition of women is a significant factor in the general welfare of entire populations?
3. Is shelter a basic human right? If so, what should be done about homeless people and street children? What social values are reflected in their plight? How might more public participation by women affect such values?

4. Why is the equality of women, and the elimination of discrimination against them, so relevant to the achievement of a peaceful world? How has the United Nations Decade for Women affected women in your society?

5. What effect has the UN Convention on the Elimination of all Forms of Discrimination against Women had in your country since it entered into force in 1981? What more needs to be done?

## Chapter 7 : Achieving visibility

1. What is meant by the 'invisibility' of women? How many of the women in your country participate in governmental and inter-governmental policy-making bodies? Why might women be reluctant to aggressively pursue political careers?

2. Why does discrimination against women start from birth and have such a devastating effect upon the girl child?

3. In what ways do advertising images affect the way in which women are regarded? How do films and media deal with attitudes toward women?

4. Has your government established national machinery for the promotion of the equality of women, as recommended in the Forward-looking Strategies adopted at the UN's World Conference in Nairobi?

5. What must be done to achieve full participation of women in the decision-making process, locally, nationally and internationally? What is the role of the UN Commission on the Status of Women, and of the UN Division for the Advancement of Women? What is CEDAW?

## Chapter 8 : Women in action

1. Name three women who have won the Nobel Peace Prize. Can you give the names of others who have been prominent in the women's peace movement?

2. Who is said to have initiated the idea for a nuclear freeze? Who made it a major international compaign?

3. What happened at Greenham Common? What motivated the demonstrators?

4. How have women writers and researchers contributed to the women's peace movement?

5. What is meant by 'the feminine approach to problem-solving'? Do you consider that women's negotiating skills are of special value in conflict situations?

## Chapter 9 : Working towards a non-violent world

1. In which ways have women been active in the attempt to achieve a non-violent world? What kind of organizations and groups have been estab-

2.  Why have women insisted that working for a peaceful world also means the achievement by women of the full and fair enjoyment of human rights as set forth in the United Nations Charter?

3.  Why are women so active in peace education? and why is it considered such an important part of efforts to eliminate aggression and violence in society? What do you believe should be the content and purposes of education for non-violence?

4.  What themes, subject matter and types of teaching do you think appropriate at each level of education? Should they include conflict resolution? What should be done about textbook stereotyping?

5.  What is the role played by toys and games, sports, television and the media, in the stimulation of violence in society?

## Chapter 10 : Making the connection

1.  Women's contribution to the promotion of peace, social equity and global development has been praised by many famous people.  Name one, and explain the occasion.

2.  Why do women's non-governmental organizations hold a special NGO forum at UN conferences such as that in Nairobi in 1985? What impact does this have?

3.  Which non-governmental organizations (NGOs) in your community and/or country are concerned with women's issues, which with peace issues? Which can provide information and education materials connected with the themes dealt with in this book?

4.  What steps can be taken by the individual to participate in efforts to achieve equality for women and a peaceful society? What might be done to encourage women to run for public office?

5.  Why is the monitoring of governmental promises undertaken at international conferences, and of their ratification and implementation by national parliaments, so important?

# Index

*A Window onto the Future*, 140
AAWORD (Association of African Women for Research and Development), 122
Abzug, Bella, 72
Addams, Jane, 119, 120
Afghanistan, 4, 39
Africa, 30, 46; African National Congress (ANC), 31, 32
Agenda for Peace, 12
Albania, 6, 85
Algeria, 3, 34
Alliance of Poor Farmers, 22
American army women, 63; inspectors, 66; American-made arms, 54
Amneh, 61
Amnesty International, 20, 22, 25, 32, 62
Anar, Meryem C, 28
Angola, 3, 15, 39
anti-war coalitions, movement, 53, 123
apartheid, 30, 31, 35, 61, 96, 106, 109, 133, 137
Apple Computer, 74
Arab culture, 56; States, 33, 58, 65, 137
Arab–Israeli peace agreement, 34
Arab–Jewish friendship, 137
Arafat, Yasser, 32
Argentina, 8, 20, 41, 124
Aristophanes, i, 118
armaments/arms: 2, 9; bazaar, dealers, 15, 54; control, limitation, 1, 15, 83; expenditures, 47, 77, 80, 121; exporters, importers, 42; manufacturers, 64; negotiations, 122; production, 123; proliferation, 76; race, 40, 121–2, 126, 128, 133, 145, 149; sales, trade, transfers, 39, 71–2, 75, 76, 83, 125
Armenia, 5, 23
Ashrawi, Dr Hanan, 62
Asian: labour, 60; women, 8, 59, 108

Aspin, Les, 13
attitudes, attitudinal change, 44, 79, 91, 140, 147
Augsberg, Anita, 119
Aung San Suu Kyi, 119
Australia, 19, 33, 52, 62, 114, 118, 123, 139
Azerbaijan, 4, 5, 23

Baker, James, 15
Balch, Emily Greene, 119, 120, 133
Ball, Nicole, 48
Bangladesh, 22, 57, 59
Belgian Jewish Secular Cultural Community Centre, 136
Bennett, Lynn, 102
Berlin Wall, 39
Bernstein, Hilda, 31
Berry, Angela, 29, 30
Black Sash movement, 33
Blanca, Antoine, 6
Bonner, Hypatia Bradlaugh, 157
Bosnia-Herzogovina, 6, 24, 65
Boulding, Elise, 18, 43–4, 118, 127, 133, 140
Boutros-Ghali, Boutros, 12, 85
Brazeau, Ann, 27
Brazil, 8, 41
Brock-Utne, Birgit, 101, 118, 139–40, 142, 145
Brulon, Angélique, 19
Burma, 119
Bush, George, 14, 16, 51, 56, 63, 65, 80, 85; Administration, 9

Cable News Network (CNN), 57
Caldicott, Helen, 123
Cambodia, 4, 15–16, 39
Camdessus, Michel, 80
Canada, 81, 114
Carter, Jimmy, 89
Catholic women in Northern Ireland, 130
Central Intelligence Agency (CIA), 54
Centre for Defence Studies, 6

Chazov, Dr Eugene, 47
chemical weapons, 11, 41, 83; Convention, 11, 15; destruction, 83
Childers, Erskine, 12
Chile, 19
China, 20, 42, 48, 51
Churchwomen United, 121, 138
Gilligan, Carol, 107, 129
civil: disobedience, 151; disturbance, 18, 38, 85, 127; war, 91, 94
Clarke, Michael, 6
Clark, Ramsey, 51
Cold War, i, 7–9, 14, 38, 39, 47, 69, 81–2
Colombia, 22, 51
Commonwealth of Independent States, 7, 76
comprehensive test ban treaty, 7, 83, 121
Conference on Security and Cooperation in Europe (CSCE), 81, 83, 114
Conference of Women in Europe in Action for Peace, 122
conflict: 138, 149, 151; prevention, 86; pyramid, 127; resolution, 2, 49, 112, 127, 134, 138–9, 144–5; situations, 90, 130, 134
Conners, Jane Frances, 101, 114
Consultative Council (Majlis Ashoura), 63
Convention on Equal Remuneration for Men and Women Workers for Work of Equal Value (ILO), 88
conventional arms/weapons, 7, 42; reduction treaty, 39; transfers, 2, 83
Corrigan, Mairead, 119, 124
Costa Rica, 79, 141
Council of Europe (C of E), 81–3
credit, 94–5, 98
Croatia, 5, 24, 85
Cruise missiles, 123, 124
cultural education, patterns, stereotypes, 82, 103, 140, 143
curfews, 32, 61
Curie, Marie Sklodowska, 119
Cyprus, 3, 130
Czechoslovakia, 42

DAWN (Development Alternatives with Women for a New Era), 122
debt burden, crisis, 41, 46, 71, 78–9, 90
decision-making, 72, 105, 110–11, 114, 134, 150
defence: budgets, contractors, 48, 68, 71, 74; strategies, expenditures, 45
democracy, 46, 62–3
Denmark, 142
Deonna, Laurence, 122
developing countries, 41, 46, 69, 71, 77, 79, 85, 89–92, 97
development, 57, 68–9, 71, 73, 76–8, 94, 96–7, 105–6, 122–3, 128, 130, 135, 145, 147, 149–51; education, 140; participatory, 78; planning, 27; unequal, 110
disappearances, 'disappeared', 20, 25, 42, 109, 124
disarmament, 1, 2, 7, 11, 15, 68, 76–7, 79, 83, 105, 110, 112, 120, 122–3, 126, 134, 138, 145, 147, 156; Conference, 11; education, 140; negotiations, 120, 122; research, 127
discrimination, 7, 19, 88, 90, 94, 136, 138, 149, 154
Djibouti, 28
domestic: workers, 98, 107–8; violence, 106, 115

early warning of potential conflicts, 13, 82, 85
Earth Summit, 41, 72
East European states, 7, 69, 81–2
economic: competitiveness, 126; distortion, 13; conversion, 73–4, 76, 83, 156; crisis, 74, 82, 95; development, 47, 109; exploitation, 44, 96, 103; sanctions, 62
economic and social equality, justice, 79, 95–6, 106, 133, 135
education: for peace and non-violence, 10, 40, 43, 46–7, 68–9, 75, 77, 82, 91, 93–4, 98, 103, 113–4, 138–9, 145–6, 157; subsidies, 90; enrolment gap, 69, 93
Egypt, 51

Eisenhower, Dwight, 80
El Salvador, 3, 15–16, 124
Elworthy, Scilla, 44, 126–7
Engels, Friedrich, 101
environment, 11, 41, 50, 52–3, 69–70,
    81–2, 135, 139, 147
equality, 78, 95–6, 99–100, 105, 109–
    11, 130, 135–6, 139, 150–1, 154,
    157; education, 140
Eron, Leonard, 143
Estrada, Carmela Ferro, 25
Ethiopia, 3–4
ethnic: cleansing, 25, 85;
    communities, 13, 101, 135;
    conflict, 18, 38, 82
European Economic Community
    (EEC), 6, 82, 84
European Movement of Women
    against Nuclear Armament, 120
Exxon Valdez, 70
Eysenck and Nias, 143

family: conflicts, violence, 16, 44, 47,
    94, 114, 141–2; life, education,
    114, 141; planning, 75, 93
Federal Republic of Germany, 42
Figuer, Thérèse, 19
food, 94; aid, 91; allotments, 80;
    distribution, imports, prices,
    production, subsidies, security,
    90–1
foreign: military installations, 124;
    occupation, domination, 35, 106,
    109; reserves, 41; workers, 57
Forsberg, Randall, 121, 126
Forward-looking Strategies for the
    Advancement of Women, 89, 105,
    129, 150, 154
France, 8, 42, 50, 65
French nuclear-testing in the Pacific,
    123

Galbraith, John Kenneth, 64, 68
Galtung, Johan, 133
Game of Disarmament, The, 127
Gandhi, Mahatma, 18, 152
Gaza, 32–3, 61, 137
Georgia, 4
Germany, 48, 81

global: development, 149;
    perspective, 133; resources, 46,
    70; military spending, 40;
    security, 88, 91
Gob Wein, 4
Golan Heights, 34, 64
Goldstein and Arms, 141
Gonzalez, Henry, 51
Grant, James, 24
grassroots: activists, 109, 122;
    consciousness-raising, 122
Great Depression, 80
Greece, i, 5, 85, 118
Greek Cypriot women, 130
Greenham Common, 123–4
Grenada, 89
Guevara, Che, 19
Guildford Four, 20
Gulf of Aden, 4
Gulf War, 2, 8, 11–13, 16, 18, 33, 41,
    43, 49–50, 54–5, 58–9, 61–5, 70,
    83, 137

Harden, Blaine, 6
Harvard, 107
health, 40, 46–8, 58, 62, 69, 75, 80,
    82, 90–2, 93–4, 98
health-care centres, 50, 75, 91
Helsinki: Final Act of 1975, 84;
    Watch, 5
Hersh, Seymour, 54
Heymann, Lida Gustava, 119
Hiatt, Fred, 75
Hickey, Tony, 3
Hiroshima, 120
Holliday, Laurel, 143–4
Hong Kong, 20
housing: homelessness, 10, 41, 47, 80,
    95; credit schemes, 95
Hughan, Jesse Wallace, 120
Human Chain for Peace, 53, 137
human rights, 1, 15, 31, 33, 43, 48,
    62, 68, 82–4, 88–90, 94, 97, 99–
    100, 103, 109, 112, 134, 140, 145,
    147, 149; education, 140
Hungary, 82
hunger, 90, 92, 149
Hussein, King of Jordan, 50
Hussein, Magdy Ahmed, 62
Hussein, Saddam, 33, 54–8, 64

India, 8, 41, 48
industrial: disputes, 138; workers, 97
industrialized countries, 10, 48, 71, 80, 85, 89–90, 92, 93
infant and baby milk processing facility, 51
Inkatha Party, 31
Institute for Defense and Disarmament, 126
Institute of Social Studies in The Hague, 108
Institute for Training in Non-Violence, 126
intergovernmental organizations, 109, 140, 150
International Atomic Energy Agency (IAEA), 8
International Committee of the Red Cross, 4
International Congress of Women, 119
International Convention against Discrimination in Education, 89
International Council of Jewish Women, 147
International Council of Women, 147
International Court of Justice, 13, 53, 85, 112
International Decade for Women, 95
International Labour Organization (ILO) labour standards, 133
International Law Commission, 112
International Monetary Fund, 48, 80, 90
International Peace: and Arbitration Association, 119; Bureau, 118; Congress, 118; Festival, 123; Research Association's (IPRA) Commission on Peace Education, 144
International Physicians for the Prevention of Nuclear War (IPPNW), 47
International Symposium on Children and War, Finland, 23
International Women's: Day, 11, 53, 73, 120, 122, 150; Decade Conference, Copenhagen, 121; Peace Camp, Geneva, 122; Peace

Movement, 118; Suffrage Alliance, 119
Inter-Parliamentary Union (IPU), 112
Inayatullah, Dr Attoya, 92
Iran, 7–8, 20, 41, 54–5, 58, 61, 64, 66, 70
Iran–Iraq war, 54, 55, 61
Iraq, 8–9, 13, 41, 23, 50, 51, 54, 55–60, 62, 64, 65–6, 83, 89, 137; 'equivalents', 13
Iraqi Women's Federation, 137
Irish Peace Women, 124
Irving, Washington, 38, 118
Israel, 9, 32–4, 41, 52–4, 60–2, 64–5, 89, 130, 136–7
Israeli women activists, 33, 136
Israeli-occupied territories, 19, 32, 61, 137
Israeli–Palestinian conflict, 64, 136, 137; women's groups, 33; Women's Peace Conference, 137
Italy, 19, 42, 52

Jabir, Sheikh, 63
Jacobs, Aleta, 119
Japan, 10, 21, 48, 52, 81, 123
Jerusalem, 32–4, 130, 136, 137
Jewish: immigrants, 137; peace activists, 33; settlements, 32
Joint Palestinian/Israeli Women's Coordinating Committee, 136
Jordan, 34, 54, 57, 59

Kekkonen, Helena, 122, 140
Kennedy, John, 80
Kenya, 4
Khmer Rouge, 4
Klerk, President, 31
Kola, Pich, 29
Kollontay, Alexandra, 120
Kouchner, Bernard, 12
Kosovo, 6, 85
Kozyrev, Andrei, 7
Krauthammer, Charles, 13
Krohne, Kay, 19
Krüger, Augusta, 19
Krupskaya, Nadezhda, 120
Kurdistan, 58, 66
Kuwait, 23, 50, 54–60, 63, 70, 137
Kyi, Aung San Suu, 119

Latin America, 46, 93
Lebanon, 19, 23, 34, 64–5, 89, 146–7
Lewis, Stephen, 51
Linkkonen, Marjo, 118
Liu Xiuying, 152
Lown, Dr Bernard, 47
Luxemburg, Rosa, 120

Macedonia, 85
McGeough, Paul, 60
McLean, Scilla, 126
McNamara, Robert, 48
Mahler, Dr Halfdan, 92
Major, John, 14–15
malnutrition, 29, 46, 58, 78, 80, 91–2, 149
Malta, 147
Mandela, Nelson, 31
Martin, Susan Forbes, 28
Marx, Karl, 101
Mauritania, 23
media, 107, 142–4; campaigns, education programme, 156–7
Melman, Seymour, 74
Middle East, 54, 56, 62, 70
militarism, i, 38, 39, 43, 120, 123–4, 128, 133, 153, 157
militarization, 2, 18, 38, 39, 69
military: bases treaty, 52, 123; budgets, contracts, 40, 74, 81, 156; contingents, 12; establishment, 14; exercises, 123; expenditures, 9, 10, 13, 40,, 42, 46–8, 68, 72–3, 75–6, 76–80, 83, 95; laboratories, 74; mind-set, 14; occupation, 48, 64; policies, values, ideology, 38–9, 69, 125; production, 7, 70, 75; repression, 38; stockpiles, 8
military–industrial complex, 13, 76, 80
Mische, Gerald, 112
Miyazawa, Kiichi, 21
monitoring, 65, 85, 103, 113
Moodley, Mary, 31
Mother Theresa, 119, 122
Mother's Front (Sri Lanka), 124
Mount Fuji, 123
Mozambique, 3
Mukerji, Vanita Singh, 26

Musawi, Sheikh Abbas, 65
Muslim: communities, 6, 146; Azerbaijani, 6; fundamentalism, 34; Sunni, Shiite, 66
Myanmar, 22, 119
Mygatt, Tracy, 120
Myrdal, Alva, 119, 127

Nagasaki, 120
Nagorno-Karabakh, 5
Nairobi, Forward-looking Strategies, 89, 95, 101, 110–1, 113, 133–5, 138, 151
Namibia, 3, 15
Nathan, Abe, 62
Negro, Marilyn, 22
Network of Asian–Pacific Women for Peace, 124
New Zealand, 118, 142
Nicaragua, 3
non-governmental organizations (NGO), 72, 77, 100, 109, 115, 133, 140, 144, 146–7, 105, 150–1, 153–4, 156
non-violence, 97, 106, 115, 134, 138–40, 149; movement in India, 151
non-violent: attitudes, techniques, 118, 141; conflict resolution, 31, 138, 149; protests, demonstrations, strikes, 124
Nordic Women for Peace, 121, 124
North Atlantic: Assembly (NAA), 81–3; Cooperation Council (NACC), 82; Treaty Organization (NATO), 73, 81–2, 121, 127
North Korea, 14, 41, 48
Northern Ireland, 124, 130
Norway, 101, 142
Nossiter, Bernard, 80
nuclear: accident, 126; arms policies, 123; confrontation, i; disarmament, 11; freeze, 121; proliferation, 7, 9, 39, 79, 83; submarines, 8; testing, 8, 72; war, warheads, 125–6, 145; waste dumping, 83; weapons, decision-making, 7–8, 44, 72, 83, 109, 127
Nusseibeh, Dr Sari, 62
nutrition, 75, 91–2, 102; deficiency diseases, 30, 92

occupied territories, 32, 34–5, 61, 136–7
Ogata, Sadako, 84
Organization of Petroleum Exporting Countries (OPEC), 55
Orthodox Macedonians, Serbs, 6
Osirak reactor, 9
OXFAM, 46
Oxford Research Group, 44, 126

Pakistan, 9, 41, 48, 57
Palais des Nations, Geneva, 11
Palestine Liberation Organization (PLO), 33, 57, 60, 137
Palestinians, 32–4, 57, 59, 60–3, 65, 130, 136–7
Palestinian delegation, negotiators, 34, 62
Pan-Arab Women's Solidarity Association, 137
Panama, 14, 89
Papandreou, Margarita, 53, 73, 79, 125
participation/partnership, 79, 97, 106, 109, 111, 113–4, 149, 154
pass laws (South Africa), 30–1
peace, 48, 96, 105–6, 110, 120, 130, 145, 150–1, 157; activists, 44, 73, 119–20, 139, 147; campaigns, demonstrations, 52, 121–2, 124; camps, congresses, 119, 123–4, 146; conference, 136; dividend, 69, 79, 81, 83, 156; education, 138–41, 144–5, 147, 157; enforcement units, 13; movement, 121, 123, 126, 128, 133; negotiations, 62; petition, 119, · 138; policies, 156; preservation, promotion, 149–50; research, 126, 129; studies, 138, 145
Peace: Messengers, 147; Net, 33, 136; Now, 53, 137; Prize-winners, 119; Tent, 151
peace-keeping, 3, 5, 12, 15–16, 53, 58, 76, 85, 127, 140, 156
peace-making, 12, 15, 85–6, 127, 140–1, 144, 151; in the family, 130
Pear, Robert, 80
People's Liberation Army, 124
Peréz de Cuéllar, Javier, 1, 2, 84, 100, 149–50
Philippines, 14, 22, 123, 142
Pietilä, Hilkka, 109
Pisango, Maria Guinarita Pisco, 25
Poland, 42
Pomerance, Josephine, 121
population: control, 46–7, 65, 69, 93–4, 101, 110
poverty, 16, 46–8, 68–9, 71–2, 77, 79, 89–90, 96, 106

Qingdao Women's Federation, 152

Rabin, Yitzak, 34
Rama Rao, Lady, 119
racial: discrimination, racism, 7, 30, 35, 96, 101, 106, 109, 139, 153; and sexual equality, 139
Racimorski, Marica, 24
Rambo, 143
Rankin, Jeannette, 119
rape: and abduction, 18, 21, 27–8, 106; and prostitution, 28
Reagan Administration, 54, 80
Reardon, Dr Betty, 128, 140
reconciliation of opposing views, 107, 130, 136
refugees, 26–30, 32, 57, 59, 61, 65, 84, 113
Richardson, Carole, 20
right: to development, 135; to economic and social security, 71, 89; to food, 89–90; to health, 89, 92; to work, 94; to vote, 100
Rio de Janeiro, 41, 72
*Role of Women in Development of Peace Research*, 127
Romer, Marta, 52 ·
Royal Institute of International Affairs, 6
Russians (immigrants, scientists), 8, 14, 33, 75, 81

Salt March, 151
sanctions, 50, 52, 56–7, 64, 99
Sarajevo, 5, 6, 24
Saudi Arabia, 7, 51, 54, 59, 62–3, 66
Scarlott, Jennifer, 9
Schlesinger, James R, 13
Schwarzkopf, General, 55

Schwimmer, Rosika, 119
second-class citizens, 32, 62, 107
security: analysis, 12, 44, 69, 76–8,
  81, 112, 129, 145, 156;
  architecture, clubs, 81; policy,
  134, 156; settlements, 34
Senegal, 23
Serbia, 5, 24–5, 85
sexism, 106, 128, 139
sexual: and emotional abuse, 21, 28,
  106; exploitation, 28, 108;
  harassment, 19, 31, 106, 138;
  stereotypes, 107
Shaposhnikov, Yevgeni I, 76
Shelley, Nancy, 139, 140
Shibokusa, 123
Silkwood, Karen, 123
Sisulu, Albertina, 31
Sivard, Ruth Leger, 2, 39–43, 47, 70,
  75, 90, 93, 126
social: disturbance, unrest, 90, 94;
  equity, justice, 79, 96, 103, 126,
  135, 139, 149–50; infrastructures,
  programmes, 40, 81; patterns
  reinforcing violence, 144;
  progress, 109, 157
socio-economic: development, 57–8,
  77, 79, 98; justice, 149; status,
  legal rights, 96–7
Soghanalian, Sarkis, 54
Somalia, 3–4, 23
South Africa, 30–3, 41, 56, 130
South Asia, 46
South Korea, 21
Soviet Union (ex-), 2, 4, 6–7, 10, 14,
  39, 41, 50–1, 54, 69, 75, 81–2, 147
Spain, 52
Sri Lanka, 3, 124, 130
*State of the World's Children 1992*,
  35
Stepanakert, 5
structural: adjustment programmes,
  90, 95; violence, 16, 38, 44, 71, 89,
  106, 108, 133, 149
sub-Saharan Africa, 46, 98
Sudan, 3
Suttner, Bertha von, 119
Sweden, 121, 142, 145
Switzerland, 42
*Sydney Morning Herald*, 52, 60

Syria, 8, 34, 66

Taiwan, 41
Tambo, Oliver, 31–2
Teachers for Peace, 147
television: advertising, 144; images,
  violence, 107, 143–4, 153, film
  producers, 143
Teller, Edward, 81
Telugu, 102
Tereshkova, Valentina, 120
Thailand, 4, 108
Thompson, Allan, 46
Third World, 39, 41, 43, 46–7, 69,
  71, 79, 90, 122; debt, 47;
  expenditure on armaments, 71
Thorssen, Inga, 73, 112, 121
Tianenmen Square, 20
torture: 16, 20, 34–5, 42, 106, 109;
  toys, 142
toys, toy guns, 107, 115, 141–2, 147
Truman, Harry, 80
Truong Than-Dam, 108
Tsubame, 75
Turkey, 22, 62, 66
Turkish Cypriots, 130
Tyler, Patrick E, 14

Udtohan, Teresita, 22
Union of Arab Mayors, 53, 137
United Kingdom, 13, 42, 65, 119
United Nations, 3, 5–9, 12–13, 15,
  30, 32, 39, 46, 49–50, 52–3, 63,
  65, 68, 72, 76–7, 83, 85–6, 95,
  105, 110, 115, 133, 138, 147, 150,
  156–7
UN: barricades, 65; bureaucracy,
  112; delegations, 154; human
  rights bodies, 112; 'interferences',
  84; machinery, 85; member states,
  56; military action, 13; peace-
  keeping force, 15, 65, 105, 130;
  presence, 84; resolutions, 65, 66;
  sanctions, 64; staff, 58, 110, 112–
  3; system, 110, 112–3, 121;
  women's peace brigades, 127
UN Charter, 6, 9, 15, 49, 52, 66, 88,
  100, 108–112, 150, 157
UN Children's Fund (UNICEF), 24,
  35, 62, 101, 145, 146

UN Centre for Social Development and Humanitarian Affairs, 115
UN Commission on Human Rights, 84
UN Commission on the Status of Women, 97, 113, 115
UN Committee on the Elimination of Discrimination Against Women (CEDAW), 99, 112, 115
UN Committee on the Elimination of Racial Discrimination, 112
UN Committee against Torture, 112
UN Conference on Disarmament, 11, 122
UN Conference on Environment and Development (UNCED), 41, 72
UN Conference on Relationship Between Disarmament and Development, 76-7
UN Convention on the Elimination of All Forms of Discrimination Against Women, 97, 112, 134, 153
UN Convention on the Political Rights of Women, 88
UN Decade for Women (Equality, Development, Peace), 96, 105, 112-3, 135, 147, 150, 156
UN Declaration on the Participation of Women in Promoting International Peace and Cooperation, 35, 109
UN Development Decades, 78
UN Development Programme (UNDP), 47, 130
UN Division for the Advancement of Women, 115
UN Economic and Social Council (ECOSOC), 34, 113
UN Educational, Scientific & Cultural Organization (UNESCO), 24, 111, 122, 145; Conference on Disarmament Education, 145; Prize for Peace Education, 122; Recommendation, 145
UN Expeditionary Forces, 127
UN Expert Report on Economic Conversion, 73
UN General Assembly, 11, 34-5, 83, 88

UN High Commissioner for Refugees (UNHCR), 4, 26-8, 84
UN Military Staff Committee, 64
UN Office in Geneva, 122
UN Relief and Works Agency (UNRWA), 61
UN Secretary-General, 1, 12, 84-5, 100-1, 113, 122, 149
UN Security Council, 5, 9, 12, 14, 16, 51-2, 56, 58, 64, 85, 100, 112
UN Treaty on Non-Proliferation of Nuclear Weapons (NPT), 8
United States of America, 3, 9, 10, 13-14, 16, 19, 22, 33, 39, 41-3, 50-2, 56, 58, 63, 65, 74, 76, 80-2, 89, 118, 121, 123, 127, 142-3
US: aid to Iraq, 54; export law, 54; presidential elections, 65
US Congress, 15, 51, 119, 138
US Defense Department, 19, 50, 74
US National Women's Conference to Prevent Nuclear War, 125
US State Department, foreign policy, 55, 89
Universal Declaration of Human Rights, 31, 89, 133-4
University for Peace, 141
Urquhart, Brian, 12

Van Ginneken, 97
Vancouver, 147
Vélez, Sandra Patricia, 22
Vienna, 114, 121, 127
Vietnam, Vietnamese, 27-8, 53; boat people, 27
violence, 16, 34, 38, 42-3, 65, 85, 94, 105-7, 109, 123, 127-8, 133, 135, 138-9, 141-3, 146, 151; deglorifying, 145; in the family, 30, 106, 113, 115, 147; in the media, 115; on television, 143-4
violent: conflict pyramid, 128; films/television programmes, 107, 115, 143; images, 138; parents, 142; sports, 141
Viorst, Milton, 55, 60, 62
Vladivostok, 75

WAND (Women and Development), 122

Wang Hua, 152; Zhihong, 20
War Resisters League, 120
warfare, 43, 75, 105–6, 133
Warsaw Pact, 39, 127
Washington, 7, 54, 130
weapons: expenditures, 69, 71; as
   status symbols, 41; of mass
   destruction, terror, 11, 41
Welsh women, 124
West Bank, Gaza, 32, 61, 64, 137
West Germany, 82
Western European Union (WEU),
   81–2
widows, widow-burning, 25, 102
Williams, Betty, 119, 124
Witherspoon, Frances, 120
women/s: action networks, 72; in
   agriculture, 90; in decision-
   making, 108; heads of
   households, 90; heads of
   government delegations, 112;
   heads of state, national leaders,
   107, 112; hugging trees, 109; in
   the armed forces, 18; in Chinese
   society, 152; in peace movements,
   109, 115; mediators, 127;
   women's movements, networks,
   societies, 57, 118, 122, 126;
   parliamentarians, 112, 154; in the
   promotion of peace, 110;
   perspectives, 106–7, 109–10, 125–
   6, 129, 145, 151; rights, 126, 149;
   studies, 129, 130
Women in Black, 33
Women, Militarism and
   Disarmament, 128
Women for Mutual Security (WMS),
   52–3, 79, 121, 137
Women Strike for Peace, 121
Women's Action Agenda, 21, 72
Women's Environment and

Development Organization
   (WEDO), 72
Women's Forum, 147, 151
Women's Intellectual Association
   (Qingdao), 152
Women's International Democratic
   Federation (WIDF), 53, 147
Women's International League for
   Peace and Freedom (WILPF), 52,
   69, 119, 121, 137
Women's International Policy
   Action Committee (IPAC), 72
Women's Organization for Political
   Prisoners, 33
Women's Talent Promoting
   Association (Qingdao), 152
Women's World Summit
   Foundation, 121
Woodward, Beverly, 126; Joanne,
   125
World Conference: in Copenhagen
   (1980), 150; in Nairobi (1985), 96,
   105, 111; on Women (1995), 89,
   113
World Congress: of Women, 149; on
   Disarmament Education, 145
*World Military and Social
   Expenditures* (Sivard reports), 2,
   42, 71, 75, 126
worldwide plebiscite on peace, 53;
   signature campaign, 121

Yeltsin, Boris, 14
Yemen, 4, 51, 59, 61
Yugoslavia, 2, 5, 15, 24–6, 38, 83–5,
   125

Zaire, 51
Zambia, 46
Zetkin, Clara, 120